The Romans in the Vale of Glamorgan Revisited

Author - Karl-James Langford

The Romans in the Vale of Glamorgan, Revisited
Karl-James Langford 2014 (reprint with extensive revisions)

Karl-James Langford PGDipAH (Leicester) author

Nicole Hay Artwork

Second edition

Published by Archaeology Cymru

Printed by **Integrated Graphics Ltd**
Unit 8, Palmerston Workshops,
Palmerston Road,
Barry,
Vale of Glamorgan
CF63 2YZ

Author can be contacted directly on:
karljlangford@hotmail.com
or Tel: 07751 255725

BODVOCI HIC IACIT FILIVS

CATOTIGIRNI PRONEPVS

ETERNALI VEDOMAVI

'Of Bodvoc, here lies the son of Catotigirnus and great grandson of Eternalis Vedomavus'. This stone is from Margam Mountain (SS83 88), now on display at the Margam Stones Museum. A stone dating from the late Roman period or Early Medieval Period, it is a tribute to those long distant people in our past, the subject of this publication.

PVMPEIVS CARANTORIVS

'Pumpeius Carantorius' stone, with a later Ogham Script, was found alongside the deduced route of a Roman Road at Kenfig (SS80 84), now on display at the Margam Stones Museum. Probably, it was originally erected to commemorate maintenance work along the route of the Roman Road, or simply as a distance marker.

In grateful appreciation of my children's love; for my granddad Noah, who always knew, who believed in me; and for the spirit enshrined in me by my grandmothers Marjorie and Phyllis; for Helen who put up with me for so long; and last - but by far not least - for those, for the love that Petra inspires in our hearts.

Also, for all of you who have remained loyal and believed in times when I couldn't.

Many thanks and sincere heartfelt blessings!

Karl-James

"Man does not live by experience alone,
but by transcending experience.
To dwell in the wide house of the world;
to stand in true attitude therein;
to walk in the wide path of men;
in success, to share one's principles with the people;
in failure, to live them out alone;
to be incorruptible by riches or honours,
unchangeable by poverty,
unmoved by perils or power –
these I call the qualities of a great man."

MENCIUS (Chinese philosopher), 372 – 289 BCE

Every effort has been made to trace the owners of copyright material, and we hope that no copyright has been infringed. Pardon is sought and apology made if the contrary be the case, and a correction will be made in the third edition of this book.

Also, it has been impossible to put a numbered text reference system to source quotations and areas of cross-referencing in this publication, simply due to time and cost!

Contents

Preface

A reprint of this publication has been long overdue. Many times have I been asked if I had copies of the publication for sale, and many times have I replied 'No, sorry'! Now, I feel, is the time for a reprint, with revisions, but with little major change from the original thrust of the 1996 edition.

However, it is my intention that at some future date this publication is to be re-written completely. But for now, my readers, please accept that to re-write this work will take many more arduous hours of dedicated research, and will totally change the approach from book one. However, many areas have been reviewed during the lengthy process of re-typing the complete book because the electronic version had been lost – proof positive that all electronic media eventually dies. I have changed some of the accepted thinking within Roman archaeology, and have used a fresh approach in some areas of this publication. You will find also there is no use of the out-of-date terms: "Celtic"; "Dark Ages"; "Druid" and "Silure".

Since 1996, when the first edition of this book was written, many changes have occurred in my private life. In particular, with the most joy given to my life by being the father of six children; Bethan, Owain, Emily, Ceri-Anne, Reuben and Amaya. But I have mourned the passing into the summer lands of David (I hope you're still writing the story of Megan the sheep), and also of Noah my Grampy, I deeply miss you both.

Since 1996, I have become a qualified archaeologist with Leicester University, excavated further, engaged in field-work and research in various areas of local archaeology and further afield, presented archaeology to various groups including radio and television, published extensively, and worked as a professional contractual archaeologist. I currently teach archaeology classes for Archaeology Cymru in Arnside, Barry, Bridgend, Cardiff, Cowbridge, Llantwit Major, Sully and the hinterland. I am writing for several publications about archaeological research and two other publications in other fields of research, as well as presenting archaeology to a number of groups. Finally moving on into a television presenting and acting career.

As an extra note to reader's please make yourself aware of the terms used in this publication and the dating system, all of which can be found towards the rear of the publication and enjoy reading as much as I have enjoyed researching this information.

I hope this refreshing reprint strengthens the reader's interest in the local Roman archaeology of the Vale of Glamorgan and its surrounds.

INTRODUCTION

The Vale of Glamorgan opens as a sweeping landscape situated in the southernmost region of Wales, forming part of the old County of South Glamorgan. In order to create a flowing continuity of information in this publication, I have found it necessary to include archaeological sites of the Roman period from outside the Vale of Glamorgan, that being Bridgend and Cardiff. Most of the Roman sites known in the Vale of Glamorgan are included here.

The archaeological Time-signs of multiple millennia of occupation before the arrival of the Romans are complex, comprising many Iron Age fortifications and dwellings around the coast, and further inland. Many burial chambers of the Neolithic times and countless barrows of the Bronze Age dot our landscape. There is more known about this period prior to the Roman invasion than there is about the 600 years or more after the Romans had long since departed.

Through these lengthy periods of occupation, the Vale of Glamorgan has been rich agriculturally, enriched 14,000 years ago with deposits left by the retreating glaciers, and subsequently through frequent deposits of alluvium. This rich natural wealth has allowed the human population to gradually increase to its modern day levels more rapidly since the arrival of the Romans.

It was these very Romans that realised the attraction of the Vale of Glamorgan above any other region of Wales; its natural assets, woodland, metal ores, fertile soils, freshwater springs, and sheltered harbours. Following the gradual collapse of the Roman administration in Britain from 407 CE, society took over 600 years to recover. In around 1093 CE the invasion of the Vale of Glamorgan by the Normans (with incursions for up to a decade before this date) offered improvements at administrative and social levels. With this Norman stage of occupation and throughout the continuing medieval period, the earlier Roman sites were looted for their building material, and eventually the monuments of the time of the Romans were forgotten and lost in time until their partial rediscovery in the 1700's.

Iolo Morgannwg (Edward Williams), an early archaeologist who lived in Cowbridge revived the study of the Romans in the Vale of Glamorgan at the end of the 1700's. He visited and recorded many Roman sites (some now lost forever), a record through drawings and writings invaluable for future generations, although now ridiculed by many of today's archaeologists. We believe he may have forged some information but not all.

Following in the footsteps of Iolo Morgannwg was the more professional and academic John Storrie, who discovered some previously unknown Roman, sites, and reappraised some of Iolo Morgannwg's discoveries. The most famous explorations of Roman sites by Storrie were at Barry Island, Ely Race Course (Villa), and Llantwit Major (Caermead Villa). After Storrie, a steady flow of historians and archaeologists would study and live in the Vale of Glamorgan, and particularly relevant to us, they studied the local Roman occupation. These included Sir Mortimer Wheeler, Thomas Ewbank, Glyn Daniel, Leslie Alcock, Stan Awbrey, Michael Jarrett, Gerald Davies, Gareth Dowdell, Howard Thomas, Gerald Beaudette and Brian Luxton

Although most of the archaeological sites mentioned in this publication are now invisible from the ground, many can be seen from the air; indeed that is how some of the sites here have been discovered. Countless Roman landscapes, whole field patterns and settlements have been revealed throughout the country over recent years through aerial photography. For example, the aerial photography carried out by Archaeology Cymru Ltd in 1995; it is very difficult to see some of these Roman sites through normal field work.

This book has been put together like a jigsaw, fitting pieces together in the correct places. There may be enough other pieces of information and evidence to compile a third book that will include more new evidence in the future.

This is a reassessment of the original "Romans in the Vale of Glamorgan" by the same author published in 1996, following work prior to and since publication, undertaken by the author and other archaeologists.

CHAPTER 1
PRE-ROMAN VALE OF GLAMORGAN AND START OF ROMAN OCCUPATION

Part 1a. The origins of human occupation in the Vale of Glamorgan

The occupation of the Vale of Glamorgan and surrounds before the arrival of the Romans is a complex issue, comprising many native-built fortifications and settlements along the coastal margin. There is more known about this period prior to the invasion of the Romans than there is about the period immediately after the Roman occupation ceased in this area.

The Vale of Glamorgan has benefited through the ages from the advantage held in its 200 – 145 million years old Mesozoic Jurassic Lias Limestone (such as at Llantwit Major and Rhoose), flanked by 360 – 300 million year old Palaeozoic Carboniferous Limestone headlands (such as Cold Knap and Friar's Point), both of which types yield various qualities and quantities of quicklime and building stone. Not only has there been a thriving industry and demand for the limestone over the past few hundred years, this wealthy supply was utilised down the ages by the Medieval merchant and Roman administration alike.

The *Bulwarks hill-fort, Porthkerry (ST08 66)* geology consists of horizontal layers of shale alternating with layers of Lias limestone. On this base a promontory hill-fort with triple banks and ditches was constructed around 200 bce. This site originally had an enclosed area of approximately 5.1 hectares; currently it is believed 1 hectare has been lost to erosion, and increasing year by year. The area of the ditches seems to have become overgrown at its current level as late as 1968 CE. In this area there are still visible marks in the dense grass of hut circles similar to some which can be

found in the area of *Bull Cliff* (between Porthkerry and Cold Knap *ST09 66)*.
At *The Bulwarks* the huts are up to 7 metres in diameter, egg-shaped and
numbering in the region of 25. However, these huts are later additions, as
the principle reason for constructing the fort was to protect food supplies,
and not for habitation. At the time the hill-fort was established, it is believed
that the coast was open to attack from sea-borne raiders, occasionaly termed
'The Gordel Raids'. These were performed with the use of low-lying boats
which were effective for navigating the Bristol Channel.

There are a number of large coastal and inland multivallate sites in the Vale
of Glamorgan (*Colhugh Castle Ditches (ST05 70), Sully (ST16 66)* and
Summerhouse Point (SS99 66) to name but a few). These were built around
the same time as *The Bulwarks (ST08 66)*, and irritated the Roman
conquerors of the area. However, in other parts of Britain the lowland hill-
forts have offered little evidence of resistance against the Roman invader;
archaeological evidence is scant on the ground for any kind of warfare.

Growing of the first foodstuffs in the Vale of Glamorgan would have occurred
after a program of isolated and uncoordinated deforestation from around
6,000 years ago, creating an enriched soil. The ground has always been very
fertile; its fertility is due to the soil having been enriched with glacial moraine
deposited after the Last Ice Age, which ended around 12,000 years ago. After
the ice had retreated northwards, grey soils which were rich in decaying
fauna, went on to form *deep stoneless calcareous soils with fine and coarse
silt known as* the *Marine alluvium*, leading to the creation of a loam and clay
soil that now covers great parts of the Vale of Glamorgan.
The climate between the middle Iron Age to the end of Roman rule (300 bce
and 407 CE) was wetter than the previous 400 years of the Iron Age, and
warmer by around 1½ °C than it is today, punctuated with episodes of
drought. This difference in temperature encouraged an expansion of
settlement not only into lowland areas but back into some of the uplands
also; upland areas had been abandoned since the reduction in temperature in
the late Bronze Age. However, the lowland areas, so prevalent in the Vale of

Glamorgan, were more suitable to settlement based around the new agricultural economy; the increase in arable farming was down to the loam and clay soils that were ideal for the new crops being planted. Not all of the farmers in the Vale of Glamorgan had the bonus of these soils. In the Vale of Glamorgan there is a strip of poor and sandy soils identified first by John Storrie in the late 1890's, called the 'Radyr series'. A farmer of the Iron Age choosing this soil would soon have discovered that he or she had made a grave error, which was emphasised by the droughts. Sandy soils do not retain water, allowing it to drain into streams; in a drought this is the ruin of the crop. This particular land was therefore used for grazing rather than for cultivation.

Part 1b. Ptolemy and the 'Essyllwyr'

According to Claudius Ptolemy (90 to 168 CE), the local people who grazed the land of South Wales, were called the Essyllwyr, 'the people of the Essyllwg'. The tribal region Ptolemy referred to as the Essyllwg comprises the areas we know under the old county names of Glamorganshire, Gwent and Herefordshire, and were also scattered around the lower Brecon Beacons and Gloucestershire.

The Essyllwyr (more familiarly known by the Latin name as the Silures), a fictional name given to a people by its Roman conquerors, is sadly now outdated as a name to give these people; a seemingly huge tribal grouping over an extensive area. Essyllwyr was purely an administrative title for a group of many unique individual tribes; a confederated title for the Essyllwg region. For the Roman administrators this was acceptable practice; fictitious titles for the conquered illiterate, but for the natives this would have been a name completely alien to call themselves by. These peoples, based at their tribal oppidia or hill-forts who were called and organised under many tribal titles, fought, it is reported, against the Romans with the courage of any

British native people. But the fortified sites, if used, were no match against Rome. Prior to 43 CE the many hundreds of individual tribal groups of Britain had set up trading arrangements, not only internally, but including those that reached out to all of the civilised world. With foodstuffs (grain and meats), gold, copper, lead, silver, tin and iron in plenty in the area they ruled, the richness of these tribes you would say was much admired. Those very few tribes that minted their own coinage, luckily preserved their identity. Through their various trading contacts, the Romans would have gained the impression that the island of Britain was very wealthy. However, in reality for the Romans in the long run, the province of Britannia would be a crippling drain on the empire's military resources.

Part 2 The legend of Caractacus; the struggle

When the Romans arrived in the Vale of Glamorgan after their successful rout of the native tribes of southern England, the native tribes of south Wales were described by the Romans as very warlike, and were naturally very angry at the invaders' attempt to overthrow their ancient rights to the land that was under their control. Consequently it took the Romans a period of time to break the might of the south Wales tribes.

By 49 CE the native tribal leaders of this war-torn amalgamation of local tribes and refugees had finally decided to stop its guerrilla attacks against the Romans. These local tribal leaders were believed to be headed by none less than the great Caractacus himself, the son of Cunobelinus, king regent of the *Catuvellauni* tribe and brother of Togodumnus. Under Caractacus' leadership, the south Wales tribes are reputed to have led a full-scale attack against the forces of the Second Governor of Britannia, Publius Ostorius Scapula (47 to 52 CE). This new approach from Caractacus seems to have failed and the ensuing collapse of tribal resistance in south Wales, as elsewhere, led to Caractacus legends fleeing north to the deceptive safety of Cartimandua, queen of the Brigantes. Eventually, she handed Caractacus over to the Romans in 51 CE, in return for a peace treaty with the Romans, which was alas short lived.

Caractacus and the local tribes deserve more of our attention; this will be done here through a narrative, as in reality all we 'know' is mainly speculation, based on little to no fact. When the Claudian invasion of mainland Britain occurred in 43 CE, the Vale of Glamorgan native population was not directly affected by events. Trade continued with neighbouring tribes in southern England. The local tribes, the Romans tell us, gradually offered their support to the south English tribes that were resisting Roman advances in the form of weapons and manpower. It is believed the south Wales tribes had offered support to the more unified anti-Roman peoples such as the

Catuvellauni and *Durotriges* tribes of southern England at the time of the Julius Caesar invasions in 55 and 54 BCE. But this time the Romans were here to stay, and any native military support given to the known anti-Roman tribes of southern England this time was in vain. The might of Rome directly started to affect south Wales around 48 CE.

A pleasant story tells us that in 52 CE the great Caractacus himself after his capture by the Romans from Cartimandua was recorded as being at the 'Eternal city of Rome' itself, having arrived in chains, and received by the Emperor Claudius I. Roman legend holds that the great emperor, conqueror of Britain, was sufficiently impressed by the native Briton that he gave Caractacus and his family a home in Rome. Caractacus was forbidden to return to south Wales, as a condition of his parole. Purportedly two of Caractacus' kin, his daughter and son-in-law, returned to south Wales without him.

The legend concerning the return of his daughter Eurgain to south Wales alleges that she built a fortified dwelling in the style of those in Rome. It is purported to have been constructed on the ruined site of her father's reputed home somewhere in South Wales, the legendary seat (oppidum) also of the South Wales tribal chiefs. Caractacus' nephew Ceri, who had remained in South Wales and supposedly governed the newly conquered tribes in the place of Caractacus, proved to be a good chief whilst Caractacus was in Rome between 52 and 53 CE, although there are no contemporary records of what really happened at this time.

Caractacus did not live long after he was taken to Rome. It is probable that he enjoyed his last days in luxury. Although there is no certainty as to when he died, it is surmised that he did so around 54 CE.

People reading my first edition of the Romans in the Vale of Glamorgan often ridiculed me for including the above legendary stories about Caractacus. But isn't it worthwhile to keep some of the magic of our past alive through such legends? Continuing to include these stories, my sentiments echo the following words of Brian Davies, a popular historian from Pontypridd: 'let's stop taking away the legend from our history; it's that legend that makes history interesting'. If I can find some facts relating to any of the above, they will be used in edition three.

Part 3 Roman governors and native resistance

The following lists the Roman governors of Britannia at the time under consideration. The period from 43 to 85 CE is relevant for our purposes. Governors would have continued to rule until 407 CE.

Consular GOVERNORSHIP of Britannia (the new province)

AWARDED TO		DATES OF RULE
I.	Aulus Plautius	43 to 47 CE
II.	Publius Ostorius Scapula	47 to 52 CE
III.	Aulus Didius Gallus	52 to 57 CE
IV.	Quintus Veranius	57 to 58 CE
V.	Gaius Suetonius Paulinus	58 to 61 CE
VI.	Publius Petronius Turpilianus	61 to 63 CE
VII.	Marcus Trebellius Maximus	63 to 69 CE
VIII.	Marcus Vettius Bolanus	69 to 71 CE
IX.	Quintus Petillius Cerialis	71 to 74 CE
X.	Sextus Julius Frontinus	74 to 78 CE
XI.	Gnaeus Julius Agricola	78 to 85 CE

A joint reign (or consularship) may have been created for other governors by the central Roman Authority, to administer troublesome regions of Britain alongside their co-governors; these have not been listed for the period above.

When Publius Ostorius Scapula died in 52 CE, and was succeeded by Aulus Didius Gallus, it was not a successful period for the Roman field army. At about this time, a Roman Legion had been defeated by a native force. Natives based over the border in unconquered Britain spewed forth the might of well-supplied, organised raids into Roman administered Britannia, disrupting the fabric and stability of a very troubled Roman government. Moreover, it took two further years to subdue these troublesome natives. Quintus Veranius conducted a new campaign against the South Wales tribes, during the years 57 to 58 CE. As the new governor he had renewed military resources, although there are no further details known about this campaign. Another campaign, in 58 CE, started to clear up the remains of native resistance in the Vale of Glamorgan. The tribes here were firmly subdued. Following this, military attention was transferred to North Wales in 59 to 60 CE, when the tribes there were subjugated to Roman rule once again!

The years 74 to 78 CE saw renewed action against the tribes in Wales. Sextus Julius Frontinus insisted on vigorous action as results were demanded by Rome. Publius (or Gaius) Cornelius Tacitus (56 –117 CE), in 'Annals XII', states that the Romans overwhelmed the Welsh tribes. It has been assumed that the main power bases of the Welsh tribes had been neutralised, and their military strength extinguished, around the year 75 CE. From this it is possible to make a learned deduction that the years 76 to 78 CE must have been occupied with securing the military gains the Roman military had made in South Wales by building an administrative infrastructure. This would have included building roads (*Via Julia Maritima ST01 73*); establishing a civilian farming network (*Ely ST14 76* and *Caermead SS95 69* – villas); and setting up military posts (*Caerleon Fortress ST33 90, Cardiff Fort ST18 76 and Usk Fortress ST38 00*). In addition, was the work of befriending the natives, all in the spirit of 'Pax Romana'. Purportedly, the Roman fleet berthed itself at the new military bases at Usk (*ST38 00*), and Caerleon *(ST33 90)*.

Again, we are told by those historians (the original quotation (s) lost in the mists of time) of old that somewhere in the vicinity of St. Bride's Major in the Vale of Glamorgan there were signs of a siege at the Hill-fort at *Flemings-down (SS88 76)* between the Romans and the local tribe in that area. This pitched battle is reputedly to have been at *Old Castle Down (SS90 75)* where there has been found a purportedly large Roman and native burial ground. The reason for these graves is not certain, but they were probably created as a result of conflict. In addition, in the vicinity of *Castle-upon-Alun (SS91 74)* near St. Bride's Major are three graves of Roman or native origin which date from the later years of the military campaigns in the earlier period of the Roman conquest. These graves contained iron spearheads, daggers and the remains of a helmet. This is a quite remarkable find, but it is the only evidence of the era that directly followed the early campaigns in the 50's CE.

Part 4 Local topography, military occupation and military formations

This part of the book will consider 'military Romanisation' in the Vale of Glamorgan and its environs.

NAMES OF THE SEA	POSITION
Oceanvs (H) Ivernicvs	*Off the Welsh coast, now known as the Irish Sea*
Oceanvs Occidentalis	*Atlantic Ocean*
Oceanvs Vergionivs	*Ocean south of (H) Ivernia (Ireland)*
Sabrinae Aest	*Severn Estuary*

The term "Romans" is used comprehensively in this book. It refers to the Romanised natives, as well as the Roman military and administrators in the region. There were probably no more than a 100,000 continental Romans in Britain (modern day England, Wales and southern Scotland) at any one time, inclusive of its military presence, the remaining in excess of 3 million people were Romanised natives and an unknown number of native Britons outside the sphere of Roman influence.

The geographical names above originated in Claudius Ptolemy (90 to 168 CE) Book II, of the 100's ce. The book was known in Latin as the Geographia Claudii Ptolemaei. In this book "Silures", the confederated name for the native people of South Wales is mentioned in several chapters. However, this was a fictitious name invented by the Romans as an umbrella title for all the tribes which must have existed in South Wales at the time. As the only surviving contemporary written records are the Roman ones, the other tribal names have fallen into disuse and long since been forgotten. Likewise, the South West Wales tribes were known under another umbrella title, the 'Demetae'. The whole of England, Scotland and Wales was referred to in Ptolemy's book as the area of Albion. The Romans developed this name and referred to the same island as being 'Britannia'.

The Romans first encountered the South Wales tribes around 47 ce, from whom there was extensive sporadic but all-encompassing warfare until about the year 75 ce. The northern hilly, wooded topography broken by clearings of farmland, and the southern densely wooded topography of the Vale of Glamorgan were problematic to the Roman conquest here, although they recognised that the same would be to their advantage in resources if they could secure the region. When they did so, they used it for training their troops, establishing marching or practice camps, as seen at *Gelligaer common (ST13 99), Llandrindod Wells common (SO05 59)* and at *Neath (SS79 98)*. The terrain served as a natural barrier against incursions into the Roman world, serving also to provide shelter and resources for the newly-built network of villas and various settlements. The Romans trained thoroughly for warfare. The Roman historian Publius (or Gaius) Cornelius *Tacitus* (56 – 117 CE) recorded: 'The Romans always halted for the night when the violence of the day had died down.' There are many practice and marching camps still to be found as humps and bumps in the fields of South Wales. After about 75 ce the political air in the Vale of Glamorgan was very turbulent. Understandably, sporadic guerrilla attacks from native tribesmen protected by the woodlands to retreat into, still dominant in the region, who had lost land etc would have continued. The last Roman sea-borne attack and invasion of the Vale of Glamorgan occurred about this time, probably around 76 ce. It penetrated all the river settlements of the remaining disgruntled natives, pacifying the hard core of those resisting Roman control. The Roman troops then occupied the well-sheltered harbours of the river valleys, such as *Aberthaw (ST03 66)*, *Colhugh (SS95 67)*, and *Porthkerry (ST08 66)*, where supplies could be dropped off for the troops.

The Romans now started to build 'flat-packed', wooden auxiliary fortlets (the Roman equivalent of pre-packed IKEA furniture of today), carried sometimes by vastly stretching wagon trains, but mainly and more conveniently via naval vessels. This indicates that they had prepared in advance for the invasion, and in some locations intended to occupy with semi-permanent garrisons.

The military bases along the rivers were now filled with supplies, and this signalled the beginning of the period of unbroken Roman military control over the region. A well-engineered road and canalised river network was established, cutting across the individual tribal areas and bringing with it control, administration, and a message that the Romans were here to stay for a lengthy period of well over 300 years, until 407 CE, with its Time-signs echoing through the ages till today. The boundaries of political territories were designated, with Roman auxiliary units controlling each one seen to have been established, such as the permanent forts at *Cardiff (ST18 76)* and *Bovium (SS99 74)* for example. The nature of Roman control - the 'Pax Romana'- allowed for the local tribes to become politically autonomous after a period of time, as seen at the establishment 'Civitas Capital' of *Caerwent (ST46 90)* for example.

The conquest had been an embodiment of the ideas of Emperor Claudius I, in whose honour a temple was raised at Colchester. The legendary battle of Mons Graupius against the Caledonia tribes, in what is modern day central Scotland (exact location debatable) in 80 CE, was it is believed a high water mark in the 'military' conquest of Britain. At the peak of the Roman invasion in Scotland, in excess of 50,000 Roman auxiliaries and Legionaries, originating from all over the empire, were stationed in Britain. The Second Augustan Legion, the one most relevant to us, was used in various early campaigns in South Wales, and would later become established at *Usk (ST38 00)* and *Caerleon (ST 34 90).*

It is reputed that in 75 CE two Roman legions and their auxiliary support were stationed in the South Wales region in readiness for a military campaign further north. The two legions were the Twentieth Valeria Victrix and Second Augustan, initially stationed at *Caerleon (ST 34 90).;* they may have had additional Marching camps at *Gelligaer (ST13 97)*, which has a number of locations large enough to support one legion. This total manpower would have been a mighty impressive sight, with up to 11,000 legionaries in their shiny silver armour, and their supporting units of foot soldiers and cavalry (the Auxilia), a total of 22,000, which amounted to half of the known Roman military presence in Britain. The Auxilia (Auxiliaries) were formed into three main units: the Alae (cavalry) divided into turmae; Cohorts (infantry) divided into centuries; and a group of mixed infantry and mounted troops; the Cohortes equitatae divided into turmae.

The following table outlines the manpower formation of these Roman military auxiliary groups:

GROUP	Strength (no. of men)	Divided into	LEADER
Alae (cavalry)			
turma	30		decurio
quingenaria	500	16 turmae	praefectus
milliaria	1000	24 turmae	praefectus
Cohortes (infantry)			
centurio	80		centurio
cohors	500	6 centuriae	n/a
cohors primus	1000	10 centuriae	n/a
Cohortes equitatae (infantry with cavalry support)		turmae	decurio

The numbers of turmae and centuriae in these cohorts in not clear

The incentive for the Roman Auxilia troops was that after serving as auxiliary soldiers in the Roman army for 25 years - where they were classed only as subjects (until 212 CE) - auxiliaries would be granted Roman citizenship. This honour was similar to a modern-day soldier gaining a full British army pension after 35 years service (although the benefits on offer then equate to a much longer service today). This landmark in an Auxiliary soldier's life was a very prestigious moment and included being awarded a personalised diploma of citizenship inscribed on bronze sheets (however very few of these have ever been excavated).

The following table outlines the manpower formation of a Roman Legion at the time of the 43 CE invasion:

GROUP	Strength (no. of men)	DIVIDED INTO	LEADER
Contubernium	8		
	80	10 *contuberniales*	*Centurion*
Centuria			
	480	6 *centuriae*	*Pilus*
Cohortes			
	120	(cavalry)	
Alae (Eques legionis)			
Legio	5240	10 *cohortes +alae*	*Legatus*

The standard Roman Marching Camp, the home of the campaigning soldier, consisted of leather skinned tents surrounded by ditches and a turf bank crowned with a wooden palisade. The palisade was made of posts 500mm long (spikes) that were carried as part of the Roman soldiers' standard kit; each soldier had 2 spikes along with digging tools. Most camps were a temporary affair used for as little a period as one night, or maintained by a small temporary detachment for use as a staging post. After visiting many of the local *Marching Camp* category sites with a very similar terrain, the author now believes these were initially constructed directly on agricultural land, usually on commanding ground. The use of this arable land is clear: without any surrounding shelter for attackers they could be used as temporary defensive positions controlling the surrounding area. Many of these sites – such as *Coelbren (SN86 10)* and *Penycoedcae (ST06 88)* to name a few - are today sited on commanding peaty situations, but in 100 ce they were on better drained arable land, perfect for the tentage etc. Some camps, as seen at *Gelligaer (ST13 97)*, were to become more permanent, with the earthen banks being strengthened with a mortared stone wall, stone gateways, and turret towers, and with the addition of roadways, bread ovens, latrines and even barracks. It is also not to be forgotten that maritime forces would occasionally have built temporary camps at recently abandoned hill-forts (such as *The Bulwarks (ST08 66))* alongside natural harbours, to protect their boats and supporting land forces whilst campaigning.

In conclusion, it is supposed there were to be seen small *oppidi*, or *civitas* (tribal capitals) established across the region. The several different tribes within the Vale of Glamorgan would each have had a tribal capital. There was probably one at *Caer Dynnaf Cowbridge hill-fort (SS98 74)*; there has also been some discussion as to whether *Llysworney (SS96 74)* may have been an important Iron Age centre to service the administration of the 'Central Vale of Glamorgan tribe'; *Dunraven hill-fort (SS88 72)* may have been the centre for the 'West coastal Vale of Glamorgan', and either *The Bulwarks hill-fort Barry (ST08 66)* or *Dinas Powis hill-fort (ST14 72)* may have been the centre for the 'East coastal Vale of Glamorgan'. These smaller tribal capitals were all subordinate to the Roman tax-collecting centre further east at *Caerwent (ST46 90)*. At this site, the Romans built a new capital town, the Civitas Republica Silurum, which was the major regional capital for the South Wales Roman political administration of the 'Commonwealth' of tribes. As well as standing in the historical record, the remains of this important capital are still displayed with the imposing walls and remains at the current town of Caerwent. The foundation of the civitas as a new town is recorded on a stone in the church at Caerwent.

CHAPTER 2
THE CHANGING FACE OF OUR COASTLINE UNDER ROMAN RULE

Part 1 Local harbours and agriculture

There is much to say about the Roman history and legends concerning the Old Harbour and Cold Knap in *Barry (ST10 66)*, but as in many cases, most of it is hearsay. However, let us start with some established basic facts.

In 1921, whilst a government works scheme was being established at *Cold Knap (ST10 66)*, there were several reports of there being pieces of 'red tile' cemented onto bedrock there. The reports were dismissed and building work commenced. In the same year the landscape was to change beyond all recognition. The railway embankment constructed earlier had cut off Romilly Park, and today it is only connected to Cold Knap by a tunnel. The stream was canalised, leading into the boating lake, feeding it with fresh water, all in the same year, the promenade was constructed linking Cold Knap Island permanently to the mainland for the first time in 8,000 years. The marshland of Romilly Park would now gradually become rich loamy soil, occasionally prone to flooding, a remnant of the time, the sea once came up this far. It is probable with the close proximiy of the *Cold Knap farmstead (ST10 66)*, and with the early indications of Roman tile, that in 1926 when the Lake Lido Pool was constructed, more artefacts came to light that were not reported.

Although by far not part of any pre-Roman ancient 'Greenwood' woodland, the woods today called the *'Birch Grove' (ST09 66)*, behind the *Glan-y-mor site (ST09 66)*, would seem to be reminiscent of the scene that would have met anyone in this region during the Roman period, as isolated wooded pockets. The clusters of yew, oak, ash, field maple and so on surviving locally today would have been familiar sights back in 100 ce. In these very same woods, several coins of Emperor Claudius I (41 – 54 CE) were found.

These coins have some significance as they may be related to an early phase of building at Cold Knap.

The site of *Glan-y-mor 'Official Building'* (ST 09 66) was not recorded until the early 1960's. However, earlier Ordnance Survey maps show where, several skeletons had been found close to the 'Official Building' site, but it has not yet been confirmed if these were from the period of Roman occupation. One may speculate about these bodies as Roman in origin, but as we have little evidence to go on, we should leave it there. In the area of the 'Official Building', pottery originating in Oxfordshire, some iron finds, and other coins have been found over the years. These are not significant in themselves as findings, but as with any evidence, in combination with other discoveries; as a forensic scientist would tell you, 'when all the little facts are added up they truly become important'.

The year 1622 brought evidence that *Cold Knap (ST10 66)* had previously been the site of a harbour, which was then gradually being reclaimed as farming land. The harbour site is referred to on the Evans Mouse map as "K4 of the year 1622", indicating the outline of the harbour and that it was then a cultivated plot of a farmer. The land joining the Cold Knap was also being reclaimed for farming, although it would have been prone to seasonal flooding. This became the Barry Manor Estate, which was owned by a Somerset family. Fresh water wells were also marked in the area, well situated in relation to the Roman sites. There is a further indication on the Evans Mouse map of 1622 that at some time the strip of land between the mainland and Cold Knap harbour had been reclaimed, marked with a dotted outline as K2. However, closer examination of the map in detail reveals that the prefix K2 and the dotted line boundaries of said land have been added later - the K2 is in a different font from the rest marked by Evans Mouse in 1622.

It seems therefore that the coastal strip of the Cold Knap was a focus for the Romans. Further evidence comes from the Roman fort walls at *Cardiff (ST18*

76); some of the Lias limestone used in its construction came from the *Bull Cliff quarries (ST 09 66)* immediately due west of Cold Knap, along the cliff edge. Also crop marks visible directly above a geological feature locally titled the *Bull's nose (ST09 66)*, observed by the author for the first time in 1995, purportedly indicate the site of a number of fairly small round workmen type huts. These quarries provided adequate quality building stone for facing and quoins, and would have been a supplement to the beach stone used for infill and occasional facings at local Roman sites (for example *Glan-y-mor (ST09 66)*. They were accessible for building material trade routes along the water ways. The Roman builders were particular, and knew exactly from experience the prime locations to source their building material supplies. Quarrying at the *Bull Cliff (ST09 66)* would have exacerbated coastal erosion, as with many other quarries worked at the time of Roman occupation further down the coast. Another contributor to this erosion would have been the flat-bottomed vessels fully laden with the cargo of worked stone berthed on the flat Lias limestone shelves commanded by the quarry workings at Bull Cliff *(ST09 66)*, waiting for departure on the next available high tide.

The cultivated landscape was ideal for growing corn; in places a rich loam, unblemished by the heavy clay or silt which so blights other parts of the Vale of Glamorgan. Therefore where better to site harbours for the exportation of this valuable commodity - grain - than here at *Cold Knap, Old Harbour (ST10 66)* and *Porthkerry (ST08 66)* along the rich agricultural coastal margin. These sites were presumably used as a base for taxation and day-to-day administration of the 'East Vale of Glamorgan coast' tribe. The wealth generated from the crops and animal husbandry would have made the local population rich enough to acquire property and materials to build the same.

The building at *Glan-y-mor (ST09 66)* has stimulated a number of arguments and explanations for its early use. However, coin evidence indicates that the final phase of construction occurred between 287 to 293 CE, during the reign of the usurper British Roman Emperor Carausius. Then it seems, sometime in the reign of Carausius's successor Allectus, the site was comprehensively dismantled, as indicated by the complete absence at the site of anything important enough to be reused, e.g. timber, roof tile, mosaic flooring, flue tiles, columns and bases, and so on, these having been transported elsewhere by water. The 22 rooms (one having been destroyed in 1962 whilst the Water's Edge Hotel was being constructed), although occupied by its builders, as evidenced in two rooms at the northern entrance and near it by the scotch mark discoloration on limestone blocks as evidence for cooking, the patrons never occupied the site.

The *Glan-y-mor 'Official Building' (ST09 66)* is in a class of its own; it is unique in Britain, but that's no surprise - normally little would remain of such structures so close to the shore line, with the extent of erosion that our coastlines have suffered since the Romans left, and the drop in temperature. It is certainly a military-style building linked with the maritime fleet (*Classis Britannicae*), since if it was a domestic building it would have simply carried on in use under whoever was Emperor, and this is obviously not the case. Furthermore, with the Roman civilisation very reliant on cleanliness, it would be surprising with such a unique important structure, if it were domestic, that no bathhouse has been located associated with the site, or for that matter it has no kind of defensive works constructed around it. This is unlike any of the other major sites, including those which are purely domestic such as the *Caermead (SS95 69)* and *Ely (ST14 76)* Roman villas.

The enigmatic *Glan-y-mor 'Official Building (ST09 66)'*, was very exposed indeed to seaward attack, so its use must be thoroughly re-examined. But above all it commanded an important harbour for military and domestic trade.

Part 2 Old harbours

The only details published about the Roman artefacts that have been discovered at the *Old harbour (ST10 66)* are in this publication: see *The inventory of sites and non-coin finds,* at the end of this book.

Let us take a look now at this second of Barry's Roman harbours. The *Old Harbour (ST10 66)* has many interesting features; most of them are from the medieval era. After so much disturbance in the medieval and modern periods, no Roman stone quays or buildings have survived. However, it is known that quay mooring posts that may be Roman have been discovered, more of which may still await discovery, buried under the so-called *'train graveyard' (ST11 67)* at the Barry Docks; an area which was part of the Barry 'sound' before 1884. Any wooden remains of quays or shipwrecks from the Roman period at this brown-field site would however, have been damaged beyond recognition by the toxic and acidic waste that was used to infill that area, which was still a large pond before the Second World War. However, fragments of water-worn Roman tile have occasionally been thrown up by utility pipeline construction at the *Old Harbour (ST10 66)*. The natural harbour here would have been sheltered by Barry Island. A hidden cove, it would have been attractive for traders who wished to hide their vessels from any marauding pirate in the channel, particularly in the 200's and 300's ce. When the tide had gone out, it would have been possible to walk from the location of the Roman harbour quays and reach Barry Island. It is therefore likely that there was a strategic settlement both here and on Barry Island.

Part 3 Great Water and Porthkerry

At 9am on either 20 January 1606 (Julian calender) or 31 January 1607 (Gregorian calender), for two long days, there was a great storm (some believe a tsunami, others a freak tidal surge being fuelled by a westerly gale), '...The murmuring surge...' (as William Shakespeare (1564 – 1616), *King Lear act 4* may have refered to the event), which carved up most of the coastline on either side of the Bristol Channel and penetrated inland in the Vale of Glamorgan as far as 2 miles. Such a powerful surge had the energy to create a cut off 'Castle Rock' just off *'The Bulwarks hill-fort' (ST08 66)*. *Cold Knap Point (ST10 66)* on the other hand, once described as being 'environed by the sea on all sides' became part of the mainland just as the Barry Island would become nearly 280 years later. After the great storm, beach pebbles gradually plugged the gap between the point and mainland, as well as filling the *Cold Knap cove (ST10 66)*. The bastion against the sea consisted of mainly softer Lias limestone and the harder carboniferous limestone. In 1796 there was another great storm which was equally destructive. These storms compounded the destructive effect of lesser storms in 1483 and 1584. After the 1796 storm 'a flat rock which seen at low tide showing erosion of the cliff, which is of loose shale and limestone, this had been badly eroded in the great storms.' On the Ordnance Survey sheet 109 of 1922 it was recorded that the *Porthkerry Castle Rock (ST 66 08)* was merely that, now just a 'Rock', eroded by the sea over many years; any reference to a 'Castle' was now erased from memory.

The so-called 'pebble fort' at *Porth Cerye (Porthkerry) (ST 08 66)* was used as a navigation point by the smugglers of the 1500's ce. When the southwest gales and flood tides re-opened the secret inlet of *Porthkerry Valley (ST08 66)*, they used the secluded paths of the *Cwm Ciddy (ST09 67)* after they had moored their boats in the natural harbour. The other path to the *Cwm Barry (ST 09 67)* was the main track to the harbour. The ancient harbour of

Porthkerry was then being used as a harbour again. The half-life of the pebbles at Porthkerry is 50 years; this means that it would take a significant event to block up the harbour again due to the constant erosion of the materials required.

The marshland of the *Porthkerry harbour (ST08 66)* was reclaimed as farming land after the 1600's, and in time it became perfect grazing land. This was proved in 1622 CE when Thomas Williams used the port area for farming. The marshiness of the Porthkerry Valley also had an effect on the building of the viaduct - on 31st August 1896 the two central stacks subsided during construction. Even to the present day the Porthkerry area still gets severely flooded. The modern golf course is often submerged at times of heavy rain - view this as a snap shot, just as it would have been a thousand years ago. The *Porthkerry Church (ST 08 66)* which is dedicated to St. Curig, has its origins at the time of local early Christianity in the area (some time maybe in the 600's to 1000's). Historians over the ages have suggested that ships were recorded as being wrecked on the 'Castle Rock' after the Great Storms. After the 'Great Storm' of 1483 it was given the name 'Great Waters'.

The silt and clays here were very excessive when a sewage pipeline was constructed through *Porthkerry Park (ST08 66)* in the early 1990's; no archaeological remains or deposits were recorded. The archaeology was obviously deeper than the depth of the pipeline allowed.

A publication useful to us and well worth a mention here is John Leland's 'Itinerary' (part VI dedicated to Wales) which ran to 5 volumes, was compiled over the years 1535 to 1543; it was never published in his lifetime. It was first printed by Hearne's, Thomas in 1745 as 9 volumes of the *Itinerary of John Leland the Antiquary*. In the book he describes part of a journey he made between the Sully Sound to the harbour of Barry. He describes a river, probably the Cadoxton, then he turns to Barry Castle: 'a ruin standing on a small hill', and he also mentions a causeway to the Barry Isle. He refers to the mouth of the Cwm Ciddy as being an outlet to the Porthkerry harbour, which he says was the entrance for ships. The surrounding area was thriving with grass, corn and woodland.

The following list has been compiled with the idea of further understanding the *Castle Rock at Porthkerry (ST08 66)*, looking at the cartographical evidence. The list below indicates that *Castle Rock* was important enough a feature as part of the mainland or as an island from 1542 until 1922.

The Antique Maps

NAME OF MAP CARTOGRAPHER & or PUBLISHER	DATE	STATUS OF PORTHKERRY
Christopher Saxton	1542 to 1610	CAFT [castle] with Barry Isle
John Speed	1552 to 1629	Porthkerry Castle
Pieter Ban den Keere	1571 to 1646	Not mentioned
Ortellius	1573 to 1580	Not mentioned
Ortellius	1580 to 1612	Not mentioned
Christopher Saxton (Glamorgan)	1584	Porthkerry Castle with Barry Isle
Joan (John) Blaeu	1596 to 1673	Porthkerry Castle
W. Camden	1607	Not mentioned
Mercator	1607 to 1633	Not mentioned
John Speed (Glamorgan)	1611	Porthkerry Castle with Barry
Mercator/Jansson	1636 to 1642	Not mentioned
Jacob Van Langeren-Jenner	1643	Not mentioned
Joan (John) Blaeu	1645	Porthkerry Castle
Mercator/Jansson	1647 to 1741	Not mentioned
John Seller	1658 to 1698	Porthkerry Castle with Barry Isle
Christopher Saxton	1693 to 1720	Porthkerry Castle with Barry
Schenk and Valk	1695	Barry Isle
Unknown	1729	Port Garreg
John Rocque	1750	Barry Isle
Emamel and Thomas Bowen	1750	Barry
Barry Map	1762	On Offry Bay
Barry Map	1798	Porth Carrig at Porthkerry
William Morris	1800	Barry Isle
John and Charles Walker	1830	Barry Isle

Henry Teesdale	1840	Barry Isle, Porthkerry
John Archaer	1840	Barry Isle, Porthkerry
Ordnance Survey sheet 109	1922	Porthkerry Castle Rock
Unknown	Unknown	Referred to as Chafes King ledge on top of an unnumbered amount of pebbles

Ordnance Survey maps after this period mark the Porthkerry and Barry areas frequently.

Part 4 Other harbours and Porthkerry

A Roman villa-type building has been excavated near to the modern-day village of *East Aberthaw (ST 03 66)*, which provides evidence that the *Bay of Aberthaw (ST 03 66)* may have been used as a harbour, which would have supported some limited trade. Notably John Leland wrote (between 1535 to 1543) about the harbour in a third party account of a voyage along this coast: *'From Kiddey Mouth, wher no Enteraunce is for Shippes, to the Mouthe of Thawan a 3 Miles by very principal good Corn Ground. At the mouth of Thawan Shippes-lettes may cum ynto the Haven mouth'*. (Corbett, J. A. 1972: 131).

What is the connection with the Roman period? In light of the Leland writings, a Roman trader from the period would have given the explanation for the *Bay of Aberthaw (ST 03 66)* with a more of a lively tone; a harbour and waterfront full of the hustle and bustle of maritime activity. Artefacts from the vicinity and surrounds of Aberthaw prove that it was a well-used area. The bay of Aberthaw is a natural harbour, which the Romans would have seen, essential; not only for trade, but also for other traffic between its vicus (see, *Glossary*) at *Cowbridge (SS99 74)*.

Colhugh harbour (SS95 67) at Llantwit Major, yet another victim of 'pebble blockage' because of the Great Storms, which had affected the Barry harbours and other locations further up the coast, would have been a natural shelter for ships. This natural harbour is well protected from the elements by the great imposing cliff brow surrounding it on the west and east bounds. On the east brow of *Colhugh harbour (SS95 67)*, there was also a hill-fort of the Eastern Vale of Glamorgan tribe, which could have been re-used in the Roman period. This natural harbour would have serviced the trading needs for the *Caermead Villa (SS95 69)* network, and the Roman settlement under the Medieval secular town and ecclesiastical settlement at *Llantwit Major (SS 96 68)*. Future excavations may yet reveal mooring posts (dateable to the Roman period if stratification evidence exists) in the deep silt at the *Colhugh harbour (SS95 67)*. Taking into account the coastline erosion over nearly 2,000 years, navigating into the harbour will have been fraught also, with problems due to eroded 'Stack rocks' just below the shoreline (although this would have been offset by the fact that the sea level was much higher in the earlier Roman period, on average by at least 5 metres) leading into the harbour; or moreover these 'Stack rocks' may have been a visible hazard in the Roman period - taking account of the erosion that did take place. Some of these navigation problems would have been overcome using flat-bottomed boats, mooring on a high tide, and departing on the same. There was a great danger navigating along this coast due to frequent sudden changes in wind direction, blowing ships onto the sharp rocks.

The Roman fort at *Cardiff (ST18 76)* would have been supplied by a harbour, at the mouth of the river Taff which it commanded. If a Roman fort existed at *Kenfig (SS80 82)*, it would also have been supplied by this harbour. It is likely that with the retreat of the cliff edge by up to 200 metres due to erosion a number of other harbour sites have disappeared, yet to be re-discovered.

The following story, although very interesting, is only local legend, and a great deal of this should be taken with a pinch of salt. Ceri, the purported nephew of Caractacus, became a governor of one of the South Wales tribes. It is surmised that he built a maritime trading fleet based at one or two of the harbour locations we have discussed above. This legend would somewhat raise the importance of *Porthkerry (ST08 66)* as one of the harbour locations. It is said that the name of Porthkerry derives from Ceri's name, hence 'Porth Ceri', the Port of Ceri. He built and maintained a harbour here, it is believed, and some of his sailors who benefited greatly with the increased trade from various locations in the Roman world, became wealthy land owners. It has been suggested that the native title for Ceri was Ceri ap Caid, King of the Essyllwg. Ceri, like his family, so legend has it was a devout Christian, although the original biographers of the life and times of Ceri may have used a great deal of biased licence with their faith. Furthermore it has been suggested that the first person to build a ship at Porthkerry was Corvinon, the Bard of Ceri.

Later in the history of *Porthkerry (ST08 66)*, Carausius (a historical figure that did exist) may have used the site, to berth part of his 100-ship-strong fleet, the *'Classis Britannica'*. It is debated that Porthkerry, is in fact named after Carausius. Carausius had a large powerful fleet. He set up a group of harbours for his ships along the coast, utilising existing natural and man-made sites including that in the Porthkerry valley, which was very sheltered from the elements, with its high cliffs and deep length of valley.

The governor Sextus Julius Frontinus (74 to 78 CE) made his last push into South Wales, using, it is surmised, the Porthkerry harbour *(ST08 66)* for ships, and using *The Bulwarks (ST08 66)* for the accommodation of his troops for a short period and as a supply depot.

Iolo Morgannwg, a Walter Mitty character from the late 1700's, recorded then a much larger promontory fort at *'The Bulwarks' (ST08 66)* than is found to be the case today. He also records there was a good haven for ships, and mentions a 'Great Storm' four centuries before his time. Iolo Morgannwg records that a huge part of the cliff edge at Porthkerry was destroyed in the 1790's. He is known to exaggerate, and change facts, and sometimes make them up, so his dates for these storms may be very wrong and out by a good few years.

At *Porthkerry (ST08 66)*, the imposing hill-fort of the East Vale of Glamorgan tribe, known as *The Bulwarks (ST08 66)*, (probably originating from a Scandinavian word), was constructed some 300 years before the Roman period. The Romans would have in point of fact utilised this site, as there is evidence for this through the J. L. Davies 1968 excavations. Interestingly enough, the Ordnance Survey maps used to refer to the site as *'Roman Bulwarks'*. The hill-fort has commanding views over the Bristol Channel and the valley of *Porthkerry*. The re-used hill-fort gave the harbour a sanctuary in the event of any incursions made on the harbour. *The Bulwarks* today cover a total area of around 30 acres, but may have been as large as 45 acres in the Roman period. The defences alone' particularly on its northern and eastern slopes, cover around 20 acres; with the enclosed area being around 60 metres above sea level. However it is believed that only one acre was re-used and fortified by the Romans. They would permit the natives to utilise their former hill-forts for peaceful purposes, after the period of conquest. Building up a picture of this occupation of the Porthkerry Valley, we must include a water supply that may have originated at this time, the *'Bullhouse Well' (ST07 67),* principally a natural spring.

Many Roman artefacts have been unearthed in the *Porthkerry (ST08 66)* vicinity and surrounds, bringing us to the conclusion that such finds (as referred to in the *The inventory of sites and non-coin finds*) must relate to an area of considerable Roman development, evidence supporting its origins as a Roman harbour. Much cartographical evidence also confirms this. Porthkerry is well sheltered, perfect for concealing ships from marauding pirates, just what the Roman administration would have ordered.

Part 5 Harbours

Let us now consider the ideas of the Roman harbours along the Vale of Glamorgan coastline in a collective way. First of all, the Roman harbours would have had a planned, organised, co-ordinated and administration operating them in the long term. There are many reasons for this. When the Romans made their assault on the Vale of Glamorgan, they needed harbours which they could easily defend with as little military input as possible. The military force was needed in its entirety for the conquest. Secondly, the approach to the harbours had to be rather deep and free of obstructions to allow the passage of large ships. *Porthkerry (ST08 66)* for example has advantages over *Colhugh harbour (SS95 67);* which would have been blighted by rocky seawards stacks and sand bars. They built all their settlements and harbours on set copybook plans, conforming as closely as they could to the unified image of the Roman Empire, one of the world's largest developed civilisations. Only the premium locations were chosen for its Civilisation. If there was the possibility of being vulnerable to attack, the proposal for a settlement needed to be upgraded to include defences, or the scheme abandoned. *Porthkerry (ST08 66)*, fitted into this ideal. In the Vale of Glamorgan, by the early 100's ce the Roman conquerors had pacified the three tribes here, leading the way towards a domesticated use of defensive harbours.

The connection between the *Cold Knap (ST10 66), Porthkerry (ST08 66), and Old Harbour (ST10 66),* harbour sites can easily be seen, but the siting of a harbour at *Aberthaw (ST03 66)* had a very different rationale, probably because it was the mouth of a navigable way to the Vicus of Cowbridge. However, the rationale in its early phase was probably similar to the former three locations; military supply. These three sites also had shelter, and were in close proximity to each other, and could therefore easily be defended. These important trading harbours for import and export were sighted very close to existing developed settlement structures; formed along their enclosing ridges and geography - meant that their administration would have been straightforward. It would have been feasible to offer military protection for these three locations by a small core garrison of a century of Roman marines. The *Cowbridge (SS99 74)* location offered the Romans a stronghold in the Vale of Glamorgan, establishing a major trading centre, essential for those now civilised East Vale of Glamorgan tribal people, as well as for the Roman villa network that was developing after the 100's ce.

The three harbours: *Cold Knap (ST10 66), Porthkerry (ST08 66), and Old Harbour (ST10 66)* would also have been essential to the rise and development of the British Roman Emperor's usurpation from central Rome during the period from 286 to 296 CE. It would have been in its heyday, indicated by the final phase of building at *Glan-y-mor, 'The Official Building' (ST09 66),* by around 293 CE, but would then have gone into sharp decline, as the Roman Empire regained control of Britain from usurper British Roman Emperor Allectus in 296 CE. The decline would have extended to the decline of *Ely (ST14 76)* and *Caermead (ST14 76)* Roman villas indicated in the Archaeological record at this time. These villa sites did in time recover, unlike the Barry harbours, whose decline was aided by a drop in temperature, and silted up in the 300's ce. Gradually the Romans, in the spirit of *'Pax Romana',* would have allowed the return of local control (including its own military protection) into the hands of the native populace.

In this area, the Roman military withdrawal would have been accelerated in the early 300's CE, due to redeployment of this manpower on the warring Hadrianic frontier in Northern England. As the income generated by the military fell and coinage in circulation lessened, the usage of harbours along the coastline by Roman occupying forces would have declined. This is also borne out in the archaeological record by the absence from this time of Gaulish types of pottery (Samian ware), indicating a reduction of Roman imports. Production of local homemade wares, wheel and hand-thrown, would have grown a little, to supply local demand for pottery.

Modern military men have surmised that the *Porthkerry harbour (ST08 66)* *was* more important to the protection of this region than it seems at first, as has been suggested above. Any ships moored at *Cold Knap (ST10 66)* visible from the channel were exposed to attack, unlike the hidden vessels at *Porthkerry (ST08 66)* and *Old Harbour (ST10 66).* When any number of pirates entering this far up the channel would attempt to raid ships and coastal sites, it is conjectured they may have come into an elaborate network of early 'light sensors'. A beacon consisting of a burning faggot on a metal bonfire stand sighted from a 'Signal Station' situated probably at the Roman *Glan-y-mor 'Official Building' (ST09 66)* on top of the now destroyed 22nd room, or a 'Pharos' (Roman lighthouse) sited at the *Porthkerry Castle Rock (ST 08 66),* sending a beam across the channel. This beam from one of these two stations from the Vale of Glamorgan would have been observed from a similar station based on the opposite side of the channel, probably at *Devon's Old Burrow (SS78 49).* A similar beacon at that location would have been observed from the *Glan-y*-mor signal station. On breaking the beams, any ship would be immediately spotted from both sides of the channel before the pirate ship or squadron reached shore. Being prepared and pre-warned of impending danger, a Roman squadron of military vessels could intercept them. In those days, such a beam would have been the only major light burning at night on either side of the channel; with such a prospect, the beams would have been unaffected by other light, and a very effective alarm system. It is likely that such a Roman squadron may have been permanently maintained at *Porthkerry (ST08 66),* or at a location on the opposing English coastline. Unfortunately, in foggy conditions, such a system of sensors would be unable to operate effectively. Any invasive ship or ships would not be sighted until the last minute. Such a military system would have required the co-ordination and patronage of the Roman military maritime administrators, and with the decline of the British usurper empire in 296 CE, and the withdrawal of military units from the region to assist in the defence of the empire; any complicated system of defence would have started to fail. The lack of military protection would have left the Vale of Glamorgan the backyard of Roman Britain, open to attack.

It seems reasonable to conclude that the *Old Harbour (ST10 66)* was maintained as useful for a domestic trading harbour; with its proximity to the settlement that surrounds it, and on the *Barry Isle (ST11 66)*. The safe sheltered anchorage at low tide in the sound would have been suitable for loading and unloading of goods with nearby storage (evidence of a number of sites exist). The *Porthkerry (ST08 66)* and *Cold Knap (ST10 66)* harbours may have gone into sharp decline in the remaining full century of Roman occupation with the withdrawal of its military patrons. The *Aberthaw (ST03 66)* and *Colhugh (SS95 67)* harbours would have remained in use to service domestic needs utilising the *Aberthaw (ST03 66)* location for the well-established villa network in the West of Glamorgan based at *Caermead (SS 95 69)*, and for the transportation of goods from the Vicus at *Cowbridge (SS99 74)*. It is clear however that with the withdrawal of the Roman military from the Vale of Glamorgan by the early 300's ce, but with continued monitoring from the well established Roman fort at *Cardiff (ST 18 76)*, the three local tribes - East Coastal, West Coastal, and Central Hill-fort would have acted to police and administer the harbours themselves.

Part 6 The importance and use of the harbours

This chapter will draw some conclusions based on the evidence about how the harbours were operated. What is not yet clear is how they were used, who used them and what for. There are several mysteries which first have to be solved; why did the Romans not site their harbours further up the coast: who were the employers and who were employed; where were the buildings associated with the harbours. The following suggests some of the possible solutions.

The harbours were used to offer safe haven and to trade items with Ireland, France and England. The harbours became elements of the system of Romanisation, having individual character in the spirit of *'Pax Romana'*, administrative buildings, mansions, military structure, quays, and warehouses. For example, one such structure has been indicated under the Medieval 'The Austry' (Ostry) building at the *Old Harbour (ST10 66)*. The signature for this level of occupation is not only the structural evidence, but also the refuse (such as pottery, bone and tile) that they created and the material that was generally disregarded and abandoned after certain phases of occupation had come to an end. It is this evidence that gives us a 'Time-sign' of the efforts that the Romans went through to introduce their brand of civilisation to Britain. All this evidence paints us a picture of trade in a wide range of goods. The question here is was the level in imports the same as the level in exports? We find little sign of stone ballast being used as imports to take a tradable product out, unlike as in later periods (post-medieval industrial). Trade in other words was balanced.

Intriguingly, it has been claimed that the network of harbours here was amongst the largest established, equal to any in the Roman Empire. This shows the importance that some historians and archaeologists have awarded the area. But the evidence for levels of large-scale building schemes has not been excavated locally. It is interesting to think that these harbours may have exported luxurious goods, such as gold from the mines at *Dolaucothi (SN66 40)*. But alas there is no evidence for this assumption. Much of the archaeology is buried under metres of thick clay and silt, or has been eroded away. But the harbours most definitely would have traded in commodities such as iron and lead which would have been readily available and natively sourced, and maybe small quantities of silver. The limestone itself and its processed product, lime, would also have been in demand in many parts of Britain. Local limestone was used particularly in building schemes in Devon and Cornwall. Exotic marble from the continent, igneous stone from Cornwall and Devon, and wood would have been imported for building of villas. Luxury pottery from all parts of Britain and the rest of the Roman world would have been imported for the wealthy villa households, especially Roman Samian ware from a region of modern day central France at the early phases of the Roman harbours in the 100's ce. Alongside these imports, there must have been exports of local produce from the villas' network of farms: pigs, cattle and sheep, or even locally grown barley or garden-grown herbs.

The Vale of Glamorgan was perfect for trading during this time of relative peace, with the protection of the Roman military, its harbours, and a settled native community. With a willing population that had embraced Roman civilisation, and a garrison in *Cardiff (ST18 76)* needing the support of the agriculture, the community flourished. More of the land would have been cultivated in this rich loamy landscape; the bread basket of Wales, with an increase in the quality of animals being farmed. For the Roman administration this would have provided valuable taxable revenue.

The new elite in the Vale of Glamorgan were more likely to have been native aristocracy who had embraced the Roman way of life. We see a change at some key Iron Age sites in the Vale of Glamorgan by the 100's ce; the large round huts on defended sites, that had been the domain of high status families, were suddenly demolished and replaced with Roman style structures: stone walls, with brick-built hypocaust systems, tiled or sandstone roofs, and Roman imported goods. This is born out at *Whitton Lodge (ST08*

71) farmstead, *Caermead (SS95 69)* villa and *Ely (ST14 76)* villa. The latter two sites became villas supported by a network of out-lying farmsteads; as indicated by the excavated evidence from *Barry Castle (ST10 67)* and *Biglis (ST14 69)*, would have produced goods processed locally and taken to markets and shops such as *Cowbridge (SS99 74)*, where evidence for these has been excavated.

CHAPTER 3
THE ACTIVITIES OF ROMAN OCCUPATION AND RELIGION

Part 1 Mining

There are many reasons why the Romans focussed their attention on the Vale of Glamorgan, unlike other larger regions of Wales, which are in the main hilly and inaccessible. And their length of occupation here was consistent with the length of Roman administration in Britain, some 350 years or more, longer than the British Empire lasted in recent centuries.

Whilst there was no gold that we know of that was mined in the Vale of Glamorgan, there were many locations where iron and lead mining took place. One such location was at *Goldsland wood (ST10 71)* just off the 'five mile lane' immediately due south east of Dyffryn House, and the burial chamber of *St. Lythans (ST10 72)* just north of Dyffryn House. These mines have been excavated in part, and it is clear that a settlement existed which supported the surrounding workings now crowned by woods, at the *Goldsland wood (ST10 71)* itself. The galena (lead ore) that was produced here was probably processed at a number of local sites alongside iron ore, including the nearby excavated Roman sites of *Moulton (ST07 69)* and *Whitton Lodge (ST08 71),* and as far afield as *Ely (ST14 76)* (if the cartographic evidence is anything to go by; particularly Ordnance Survey maps of the 1800's), and more sites have been indicated from iron smelting activity at *Dinas Powis (ST15 70).* Lead would have been made into 'pigs', and stamped with the local producer's patrons mark. If the patron of such metal goods was military it would have held the legionary number and standard legionary badge. Any such 'pig' has yet to be found. Smelted metal was an expensive commodity, it could not be lost un-processed without serious financial consequence.

Both the staple ores and the smelted goods ('pigs') would have travelled far and wide, and the Barry harbours were ideal for this export. Not only was there galena (lead ore) in plenty, but haematite (iron ore) was available at *Llechau (ST01 80)* and elsewhere in *Llanharry (ST01 80)* just on the north western outskirts of the Vale of Glamorgan. At least three potential sites are known where this ore may have been extracted in Roman times, mostly according to scant local evidence and hearsay. Much of the physical evidence has been lost and destroyed due to later workings of the same seams worked by the ancient Romans.

Evidence for smelting activity can be found at several higher status sites, where iron slag floors (metalled) have been indicated in excavations, for example, at *Ely (ST14 76)* Roman Villa.

The varied reasons for the Roman invasion of Britain are debatable, but it is clear that some of the natural resources in the Vale of Glamorgan would have drawn them here literally like a magnet (attracted to the iron!) They would have been given indication of such locations through trade before the invasion. Attractive too were its other natural resources such as its rich land for cultivation and grazing.

Part 2 Exports, imports and coinage

It is fitting at this point to take a look at other areas of import and export trade, and some areas of industry in the Vale of Glamorgan.

At a number of settlements in the Vale of Glamorgan various kilns have been discovered. These kilns were for drying corn *(Cae Summerhouse (SS98 66)* and *Whitton Lodge (ST08 71))*, and possibly for pottery (*Llanederyn (ST19 81)*, with others indicated in the Vale of Glamorgan having been located by the author, including one such near to *Llantwit Major* (SS93 69).Even though local pottery manufacture may have been inferior to other examples in Britain, it would still have been exported. There were also numerous ovens for making bread, sited at a number of locations as typical with any Roman site.

Trade can also be indicated by the amount of coinage that has been excavated in relevant archaeological contexts in the Vale of Glamorgan. The number of coins in the various hoards that have been discovered here is also encouraging, the *Sully Moors (ST14 68)* (1899) hoard and *Monk Nash (SS92 70)* (2000) hoards to name a few. With recently discovered hoards, presumably the individual that buried them had intended to come back, but never did. It makes us wonder how many more hoards were buried and then retrieved by the original burier. Some hoards may be caches of military pay packets that just didn't travel with the troops, who went unpaid for months. Coins from the early stages of occupation right through to as late as the 400's ce have been revealed, indicating not only trade, but also a continued military presence. It is the Roman soldiers that would have been paid with newly minted coins.

Evidence of the effort gone through to produce forgeries throughout the period from the 300's and 400's ce tells us that coinage was still important in trade. However, the level of genuine silver coinage had decreased from the

300's ce, and gold coinage became almost a rarity (just as the £50 note is today, or better still a modern day gold sovereign). This devaluation came hand in hand with inflation, and a general devaluing of money, and with it came the gradual breakdown of the economy not just in Britain but throughout the Roman Empire.

Evidence of trade comes from the findings of amphora jars on the Gower and elsewhere, proving yet again that the local population was trading far and wide with the rest of the Roman Empire. The economy seemed to be strong in peaceful times of the 100's ce, with settled environmental conditions favourable for good yields of a variety of cereals (barley, oats, rye and wheat). These cereals were taxed by the Romans through those that had created the villas under their patronage.

As well as the Vale of Glamorgan's minerals (iron and lead), wool may have been a major staple export. It would have been an important commodity for exchange and sale at the region's market places.

After the collection of any centralised or local taxes, whether as monetary or in kind (goods such as wool, lead etc), or even as labour, the money or goods in particular would have required secure storage; usually this was a strong room at a local permanent military site, such as is on display at the Roman fort at *Segontium Caernarfon (SH48 62)*.

The technicalities of who owned the Vale of Glamorgan landscape is open for discussion, but overall the powerful landlords under the patronage and protection of the Romanised authorities would have controlled a vast agriculturally rich landscape in the Vale of Glamorgan. Many of these powerful landlords were those aristocratic families (freemen) of the three main Vale of Glamorgan tribes that had survived the Roman invasion, as well as those families that had settled here from elsewhere in Britain, and even the occasional Roman settlers. These senior members of society, who also acted as administrative magistrates, lived and co-ordinated their estates from their defended villas at *Llandough (ST16 73), Ely (ST14 76)* and *Caermead (SS95 69)*. Lower status tribal peoples in the Vale of Glamorgan acted as tenants to the aforementioned landlords (very much as they would act in the Medieval period some 1,000 years later, bound to the land and the master they served) living and working on their land at defended farmsteads such as *Biglis (ST14 69), Barry Cae Summerhouse (SS98 66)* near Porthcawl and *Pop Hill (ST15 70)* Dinas Powis .

This *'Pax Romana'* society required the import of luxury goods, as evidenced by findings at the range of sites here, usually carried in luxury containers:- wine in amphora, marble, decorated tiles, and so on. Most of these goods would have been shipped to the harbours and then taken along the canalised river network to their required destinations, but certainly NOT along the poorly maintained Roman roads. It's really a myth that these roads, mainly built by the military early on in the 00's ce and used by them for a short period of time, were ever kept in a usable state by local civilian authorities (despite the Roman central authorities' desires.) Consider modern road examples that quickly deteriorate if left uncared for, even for a few years (a pathed Roman Road may even last longer than is modern counterpart).

Going by historic records and illustrations, and even by some types of tableware pottery excavated locally that were used for specific food products, a Samian dish maybe, for grapes or garum (a fermented fish sauce concoction made using fish gut and anchovies; mind you, evidence for these delightful dishes doesn't survive in the archaeological record, could you imagine the smell after all this time?), luxury imported Roman foods, including anchovies, citrus fruits, soft fruit such as cherries, African bananas and apples, and fish dishes such as Anchovy sauces were all found locally.

The wines available would have been imported from as far afield as Egypt, and closer to home from the South Coast of England (temperature being a tad warmer). The amphora was occasionally stamped, giving an indicator of country of origin, and even the producer's name! Emperor Marcus Aurelius

Probus (276 to 282 CE), finally gave permission for the native Britons to start cultivating their own vines and make their own wine, after seeing their neighbouring Roman retired servicemen and Roman settlers doing the same from the early years of occupation. Alongside this, foreign imports into the Vale of Glamorgan may have declined, and wine from southern England may have arrived in barrels, consequently leaving little trace unlike the large amphorae previous to this.

As a stab at closing this section, let's conclude with an appropriate look at Roman coinage. To gain a general picture of the values of coinage arriving in the Vale of Glamorgan; over the period of Roman occupation it is discussed here with tables. Coin locations discovered in the Vale of Glamorgan are listed in the *Chronology of selected Roman Emperors' (with important Caesars and Empress) and Usurper emperor's derivatives.*

Not all of these coins would have been minted on the continent; it would not have been uncommon to find lower value coins produced at a mint in London or elsewhere in Britain. New coinage: mint condition coins may have arrived here in the Vale of Glamorgan as payment for the Roman garrisons, then circulated from there. The coins of unpopular Emperors' would have been recalled rapidly, as a mark to eradicate their memory, and hail the new beloved (for a short time anyway) emperor.

43 CE (Claudius I) to 301 CE (Diocletian and Maximianus). The values of the following coins varied. It excludes the radiate crown coins, which were issued between 259 and 274 CE (Postumus to Tetricus II) by Emperors' of the usurper Gallic empire, and other Emperors' represented by spiky crowns sometimes worn by these Emperors' as an alternative to a wreath. The 'Radiate' was also reissued in name by Emperor Diocletian (284 – 305 CE) as a debased silver coin, typically with little to no silver content, from 301 CE. There were around 200 Diocletian radiate coins worth a single gold Solidus.

Types of coin

Name of coin Each:	Relative value was worth:
Gold Aureus	25 Silver Denarii
Gold Quinarius Aureus	12½ Silver Denarii
Silver Denarius	16 Copper Asses
Silver Quinarius Argenteus	8 Copper Asses
Silver Alloy Antoninianus (after 215CE) worth)	8 Copper Asses (initial
Bronze Alloy Orichalcum Sestertius	4 Copper Asses
Bronze Alloy Orichalcum Dupondius	2 Copper Asses
Copper As	2 Brass Orichalcum Semis
Brass Orichalcum Semis	2 Copper Quadrantes
Copper Quadrans	¼ Copper As

At the beginning of the 300's ce gold became more scarce. With the empire retracting from some regions where gold and silver was mined, such as the Balkans, and large quantities of gold being paid to third parties outside the empire as tribute demanded to secure the borders against invasion, circulation of gold coinage in particular diminished. In the latter years of the empire, gold was restricted in circulation and availability controlled. The pure Gold Solidus replaced the Aureus (which had been set in weight under Gauis Julius Caesar leadership between 49-44 BCE at 8 grams and reduced to only 6.5 grams by Caracalla 198 - 217 CE) as the main non-debased valuable metal in wide spread circulation.(Silver coinage was gradually debased by the addition of other metals within the coin smelting process and bronze coinage suffered the same fate). The Gold Solidus weight was maintained at a weight of 4.5 modern grams (a Roman libra or pound was worth 327 modern grams) of gold per coin at the time of *Constantine I* in 312 CE; as before the coins became too worn down and lost weight, now the coins would be recalled, re-minted and re-circulated, keeping its weight and value as standard.

Type of coin replacing the previous coinage

For the period: 337CE to 407CE (Constantine II, Constans I & Constantius II)

Name of coin Each:	Relative value was worth:
Gold Solidus	12 Miliarenses
Silver Miliarense	2 Siliquae
Silver Siliqua	71/2 Folles
Bronze Follis	40 Nummi
Copper Nummus	1/7200 Solidus

Part 3a Agriculture

At this point it is fitting to introduce a more detailed look at the agricultural Roman Vale of Glamorgan.

There is much evidence from an archaeological standpoint in the area of the Vale of Glamorgan to prove that agriculture was essential to the Roman presence here, and the backbone of its military presence. The field patterns indicated by interpretation of crop marks revealed with aerial photography at *Dinas Powys Common (ST15 70), St. Bride's Major (SS89 72)* and *Penmark (ST05 68)* indicate extensive Roman cultivation, (unless these are of Medieval origin). Alongside this, more substantial evidence has been found in the form of corn dryers, such as those found at *Dan-y-graig, Porthcawl (SS84 98)* Roman Villa located alongside some cultivated strips; and with various storage outbuildings nearby (such as found at: *Whitton Lodge ST08 71* Roman farmstead). With the introduction of new methods- a ploughshare, hardier grains, drainage and so on, the Iron Age plough technology was far surpassed in the Roman period, leading to higher yields and more time to extend plough zones.

Much greater use was made of the rich Vale of Glamorgan landscape, with deforestation making available larger stretches of untapped ploughable land. The new soil was then treated, usually with lime spreading to neutralise the acidic soil created by woodland formation.

In recent years, observation of field patterns has extended our knowledge of Roman cultivation in the Vale of Glamorgan into areas where we had drawn a blank with any artefactual evidence from the period. The locations at *Ewenny (SS90 77), Penllyn (ST98 75), Llancarfan (ST05 68)* and *St. Bride's Major (SS88 75)*, to name but a few, have given us a Time-sign to the intense over-productivity of farming here. These landscapes are still dominated by agriculture today; a testament to the long-held farming tradition.

There were a number of different cereal types grown in the Vale of Glamorgan in those days.

'Emmer' was originally grown into the Bronze Age and beyond, being one of the more important cereals locally because it was suited to both low and upland growing. Consequently, it was very important to those tribes of Wales and elsewhere in Britain who had dwelled in the mountainous regions, and may have moved to lower pastures in the winter. Emmer would have survived as a food source into the Roman period. It grows in light dry soils (well drained), so unlike most other cereals it had to be sown in spring rather than in winter. It has a higher protein content than modern bread wheat and so would be very beneficial.

'Spelt' was grown in Britain at the time cultural change-over. Although not as productive as Emmer, it still had potential. Spelt grew under the same conditions as Emmer, as well as in heavy soil (more clay content), light soil (more sand content) and other soils. It was usually sown in the winter, with little crop rotation, and may have been widespread in the Vale of Glamorgan.

'Bread wheat' was would have been used more extensively in the Roman period particularly in the Vale of Glamorgan, but not on such as large scale as would have been the popular experience in the Early medieval period. It grows in deep clay loams and heavy soils. It has a high yield potential, and is easily threshed. But as a downside, it tends to be easily exploited by birds and therefore it is more vulnerable than most cereals. It is also easily attacked by fungi, more so than any of the other so called 'primitive' wheats (see latter) and is very weak in its fight against weeds. More fertile soil is usually required for Bread Wheat than is required for Emmer or Spelt. The major advantage is that much higher yields are a potential major benefit over the latter two, if the farmer has access to an increased level of fertilizer and man-power. However, the high costs present a problem for those landowners, and another reason why it was not more widespread here.

Barley was in widespread use throughout the Vale of Glamorgan as it could be sown in two seasons: winter and spring, and has a shorter growing season than the latter wheats. It also ripens faster than other cereals. Barley needs to be sown in deep fertile soil which is well drained and loamy (so the alluvial plain along the edge of the River Thaw is out then!), but may establish itself well in both heavy and light soils. It is tolerant as a cereal to both saline soils (along the sea coast) and alkaline soils (soil created in chalk and limestone areas) conditions which are present in calcareous regions. For barley to grow effectively a pH value of 6 (which is the same pH as human urine) or over is required, as it is sensitive to acidity (soil in areas freshly cleared of woodland). It has a lower yield in sandy zones along the coast as drainage tends to be poor, and barley has a low tolerance here. Barley is ideally suited to most zones of the Vale of Glamorgan soils and does not need as much work for it to grow as other cereals. Barley is still grown extensively in the Vale of Glamorgan today. Barley would have been the required import of Rome, exported from our harbours.

Oats have been farmed in the Vale of Glamorgan and introduced, it is believed, in the Roman period. They are sown here today, and thrive in moist dry conditions and are harvested when unripe. Oats are sown in spring (like emmer) rather than the usual sowing of cereals in winter. Oats can tolerate acidic and infertile soils. They grow best in deep retentive loam and clay loams. However they are sensitive when exposed to the elements, especially the summer heat and excessive wet periods, alongside occasionally untimely changes in temperature, so they would not be ideal for the ever changing seasons presently experienced in the Vale of Glamorgan today.

Over all, the Vale of Glamorgan offers a diverse environment for growing the various crops of the Roman period.

Now a look at animal husbandry that the author feels may be of interest to the reader.

Cattle farming is also worthy of consideration, unlike the cereals we have discussed above, as bones leave evidence in the archaeological record. A variety of pre-roman ancient British cattle breeds (White Park, White Chillingham, Welsh Black, and Shorthorn) were available to pre-Roman people in Britain, and with new breeds and cross breeding introduced by the Romans, this variety increased. Many of the breeds in 100ce Britain resembled some of today's that truly have their origins dating back to this period. Cattle stock in Britain was smaller than today's most popular breed, the Holstein-Friesian. The cattle known to the Romans were hardier than modern cross breeds such as the 'White Park cattle breed', but this was an ideal state of affairs, as they were suited to upland areas as well as lowland areas: ideal for the Vale of Glamorgan's mixed flat in winter, then moved to undulating hilly landscape in summer. Larger tracts of the 'uplands' were available to the farmer then, due to the warmer temperature. These same cattle were adapted to handle the damp and then alternating dry conditions that even today the Vale of Glamorgan offers. 'White Park cattle breed' mirror some of today's hardier breeds such as the 'Shetland', that do not require housing in the winter (unlike today's Holstein-Friesian breed which need shelter from today's winter and spring cold weather). The Roman period cattle could graze on the local fields and could be fed in the morning by thrown food, even if they weren't penned up. They could if they were less hardy be kept in open yards and enclosures of the living quarters in the winter to stop them wandering across the 'open common landscape' and left to the open landscape in the summer. An economy flourished that was developed to see the value of local cattle, sold and traded at its markets places in the Vale of Glamorgan.

Animal husbandry

Pigs, goats and sheep, were smaller than today's breeds. The pigs and goats would have foraged in local woods alongside wild boar, and sheep grazing extensively. Sheep and goats today and in Roman times, however, would have disliked the damp low-lying land and were prone to disease if their husbandry had been poor. Generally Roman sheep were tolerant and hardy, but were sensitive to temperature and severe weather conditions. The lambs needed to be kept in warm dry shelter throughout the winter nights after they had grazed during the day. Their carcass weights varied, based on the localised climate. Obviously dry, well-drained soils, with shelter from cold winds would have suited sheep in parts of the Vale of Glamorgan (Dinas Powis for example), and their carcass weights would have been greater than in some of the damp conditions found at Bonvilston (but this is based on today's landscape). The further west and north in Wales, the more inclement weather for the sheep, that today's new breeds such as the 'Lleyn' and 'Beulah Speckled faced' can cope with these harsh climates. The damper climate equals lower soil fertility in weather-worn uplands, and clearly poorer vegetation. As you reached further north and west this would have been a great disadvantage to the Romanised farmer then, as even today the economy reflects starkly to the South and the East of Wales; that being less sheep per hectare being raised in the north compared to the south.

Pigs preferring established woodland (or similar habitats) were ill-suited to farming in the damp north and west of Wales, sensitive to the cold and damp, with more upland and less woodland, foraging and protection for the pig from the elements left them at a disadvantage clearly to the sheep. Consequently there would have been fewer pigs in areas such as the Brecon Beacons, and closer to home in the northerly reaches of the Vale of Glamorgan. Although the southern parts of the Vale of Glamorgan had a lot of green wood cover, as indicated through the fauna collections at archaeological excavations, farmers would have kept pigs. The Roman pigs were hardier than today's breeds and may have been kept in shelter at night as they had been domesticated at this point from the wild boar. Pork and hams were preferred by the Romans in their various recipes. Being protein rich, and fattening sooner, the pig grown under the correct conditions could offer the farmer a productive crop.

In conclusion, good pasture was to be held in lowland parts of the Vale of Glamorgan for the cattle, with available sheltered woodland for the pig, and grazing for the sheep and goat in other regions of the Vale of Glamorgan.

During the Roman period there was a gradual improvement in climate with an increase in the population which meant further exploitation of the land with its diversity of soils. For about 200 years before the Roman period, the localised climate was milder and dryer, with higher temperatures. However, in the period commencing in the 400's ce and after the Roman period in the Vale of Glamorgan, the temperature slowly but surely decreased and the climate worsened until it can be seen as very similar to that found today.

There was an improvement in overall temperature, where it was warmer and drier than previously, and in later years between 250 to 400 CE, it was ideal for cultivation and animal husbandry, with a subsequent rise in the 'Villa' building seen locally and across Britain. Of course, whatever is said about these temperature variations, there was an increase in the utilisation of the landscape here in the Vale of Glamorgan, and heavy ploughing enabled the exploitation of the soil, which reduced growing times. Irrigation on a large and organised scale was used for the first time. Lighter soils took longer to warm up in the spring, so heavier soils were better. The societal collapse after the Roman military control had declined by 407 CE in Britain, lead to the soils having time to recover to pre-Roman conditions.

41% of Wales is situated 152 metres above sea level, despite the popular myth that most of Wales is a mountainous desolate land. All available land would have been utilised by an organised centralised machine such as the Romans. This Roman landscape was utilised a thousand years later by extensive Cistercian monastic estates at *Aberconwy Abbey* (even with more inclement weather systems than was the case at Roman times.) This gives us the following figures that would have had earlier Roman parallels:

The landscape would have been stocked with 5 cattle heifers to every 3 sheep in 'ewe', and on the other hand 1 cattle in colt to every 2 sheep in lamb. The latter figures come about through the slaughter of more sheep before they came of age, unlike the cattle. The monastic records indicate also a landscape with 1 cattle to every 2 sheep per hectare. These details can be taken as meticulously accurate, 'the work of the lord is an honest one'. The Roman occupation may have exceeded these stock figures with the ideal conditions for animal husbandry that existed then.

The inhabitants, be they native or Roman in the Vales and Valleys of South Wales, were highly dependent on the rich crops and livestock. Being fixed to an organised landscape co-ordinated through the limited number of Villas through a highly motivated and organised network; it was important to rotate crops and grazing, to maximise output. With the storage of grain at Villa sites, these would have offset short term crop and animal failures.

Part 3 b. Agriculture and the army

We know much more about the Roman soldier's food requirements from various published texts and excavated military locations, so this is where we go next.

The following gives an indication of the rations required by the Roman Legion and their Auxiliaries as standard

For each Roman soldier daily
2 pints of sour wine (not necessarily for drinking, but for hygiene also)
2 pounds of either of the following (based on supply, demand and auxiliaries regional preference): meat, fish, shellfish (oysters), poultry, game, beef, mutton, goat or pork
3 pounds of bread or 2 pounds of grain to grind and to prepare their own bread at the forts many bread ovens
1/8 pint of oil (for cooking and bathing)

For each horse daily
7 pounds of barley
1/6 loads of hay (or barley straw)

In addition to the various cereals available to the Roman soldiers, they would have been given citrus fruits and vegetables grown in the country to prevent scurvy due to a lack of vitamin C from their other daily diet. Roman physicians would have understood the effects of a poor diet on their soldiers.

The Histories of the Greek author Polybius (203 – 120 BCE) writing long before the age of the Roman military garrisons stationed in Britain, were felt by William Roy (*Military Antiquities of the Romans in North Britain, 1793)* - to be adequate in assumption to base much about what we believe to be the case today about Roman castrametation and military life. In his writings there was a section devoted to food supplies. The work of Roy (1793) indicated that in 80 CE and for a short time after, that the 28,960 auxiliaries, legionaries and 3,000 cavalrymen (total of 31, 960 soldiers) comprised the garrisons stationed within Wales and the borders. These had at their disposal a total of 401,460 bushels of wheat; 265,390 bushels of barley, and 23,336,640 pounds of meat per annum. The same garrisons 20 years later had 350,000 bushels of wheat; 250,000 bushels of barley, and 20,000,000 pounds of meat per annum, indicative of a decrease in troop numbers stationed here to 27, 628. As archaeological evidence, the Usk and Caerleon bases of the Second Augustan Legion, were gradually being decommissioned. These food stuffs would have been sourced locally through the market place and Villa network. Then for the military campaigns throughout the 100's CE, the pacified native tribes in Wales would have seen a dramatic reduction in military garrisons.

It is estimated that across the Romanised landscape, 62 to 74 bushels would be obtained from one fertile hectare of land, but many storage buildings would be required for the threshed corn provided by the civilian villa network. A standard infantry garrison of 500 soldiers with a limited number of horses required the local villa attached to it having control of in excess of 3, 500 hectares to grow sufficient crops, and to graze their animals. Much manpower and many wagons were needed for collecting the food stuffs from the villas and delivering it to the garrison. Consequently civilian communities with traders known as vici were established around such military bases as *Caerleon (ST34 90)* and *Cardiff (ST18 76)* and the other sites in South Wales. The civilian population was encouraged to form a territorium around fort sites, creating a zone of around a quarter of a mile radius, which created the needs of the fort; its civilian potters, bakers, hostelries, homes for relatives, animal husbandry, storage of supplies and so on. These were initial stages of long term occupation.

Many cereals would have been imported if the military out-stripped local supply. Obviously the local population would have needed to feed itself, and a balance was required, in the spirit of 'Pax Romana'. Obviously as seen earlier some food stuffs had to be imported, especially during the early years of Roman Britain. Oil and wine had to be imported for long periods of time, and local native growers weren't able to mass produce wine. The proclamation of Emperor Probus (276 – 282 CE) changed things, whereby permission for this produce to be grown in Britain was granted (as surmised at *Sully ST16 68*).

Part 4 Religion

It now remains to discuss the very important heritage of the Pagan and Christian religious influence in the Vale of Glamorgan.

There are few archaeological sites that can be called upon for evidence of 'religious' activity in the Vale of Glamorgan which owe their foundation to the Roman period. Historians have surmised about a religious site at *St.Donat's (SS93 68), and* to an early Christian foundation of sites in the later Roman period at *Cadoxton (ST12 69), Llancarfan (ST05 70)* and *Llantwit Major (ST96 68)* churches, but this archaeological evidence has been all elusive. But we do have later Roman Pagan sites proven through the archaeological record established at *Caerwent (ST46 90),* and further east at *Lydney (SO61 02).* The legend for early Christianity existing in the Vale of Glamorgan in the Roman period still has to be proven beyond doubt.

But legend is enlightening reading, so we will go there for a short time. The St. Donat's location has a very interesting aspect, when looking at the history of the Vale of Glamorgan's place in religion. The now famous Caractacus was (whomsoever of our learned historians suggested this one) is reputed to have been converted to Christianity by Illud, at the eternal city of Rome itself after he had been taken their as a prize of the British military campaign, alongside his daughter Claudia Eurgain (a distinctly Roman name for native Britain don't you think!). When Claudia decided to return back to her land of birth, after her father's untimely death in around 53 CE, she brought with her Illud. Legend has it that Illud was the first Christian to introduce the Britons to this new religion. Claudia, the story goes onto to say, founded a monastic cell at *Llantwit Major (SS96 68)* close to the present day church, over 500 years before another person with a similar name to our Roman Illud; 'Illtyd'. Claudia became known as Bangor Eurgain or Caer Eurgain, such was the prestige of being the first convert of Christianity in Wales. And, yes there is more to this story, St. Paul, yes THE St. Paul probably visited Eurgain in the Vale of

Glamorgan, so we can see that she must have been pretty important to the faith to be visited by a living Saint who had met Christ. Readers, whether you believe any of this is up to you. None of it has any equivalent Time-sign in the archaeological record. The name Illud and Illtyd are interesting to understanding this early religious form of Christianity, and with a little narrative licence some historian at some point of time may have pushed and tweaked history a little.

Furthermore, these legends purport that the first Christian school in Wales was established around 63 to 66 ce at *Llantwit Major (SS96 68)*. It could even have been the first Christian school in Britain. Turning to St.Donat's also, legend tells us of a pagan temple that was converted by Eurgain into a Christian church. Dates of coins indicate some activity at this time anyway. How the builders got away with this in an environment that was clearly anti-Christian is anyone's wonder. But let's hit base here: were the Romans that against Christianity in Britain, or is this all propaganda. These legends of local Christianity are definitely worth a thought. Isn't it fitting to keep the legends alive?

But to be fair to some of these historians, it's a lovely story isn't it, 'all this early Christianity', and we will excuse them for their poetic licence. 'Why destroy all these legends', as a good historian friend used to tell me, 'let us have a little legend Karl'.

Moving on in a mist of legend, let us turn to a prime candidate for Barry's link with this early Christianity. It is highly unlikely (whether this was in the late Roman period or later) that *St. Cadoc's (ST12 69)* church Cadoxton was alongside *Llantwit Major (SS96 68)* church with an early Christian community. But some elements of a Romanised community may have embraced Christianity at the end of the Roman period or not so long after, leading to the foundation of a Christian site here, the 'Vill of Cadoc'.

Some date in the 180's CE, a senior member of the community in the Vale of Glamorgan known as Lleurwg (also believed to be the same Romanised native in the 100's called Lucius), it is purported sent two messengers: Elfan and Medwg to the Christian bishop of Rome (a certain Eleutherus, believed to be an early Church leader in the late 100's), to request for more Christian missionaries. Allegedly, this resulted in two of them being delivered to Lleurwg. These men were Saint Dyfan and Saint Ffagan. The legend goes on to say that these missionaries were very successful in converting the local population, native Britons and Romans alike, to the new Christian faith. Consequently in the late 200's there were a number of Christians recorded as living in the Vale of Glamorgan. Bishops from the Vale of Glamorgan were sent to Rome, and were apparently present at the Christian Council of Arles in 314 CE. The two saints Dyfan and Ffagan gave their names to the places in which they worked from, later to find a medieval site dedicated at each of these locations (*Merthyr Dyfan ST11 69* and *St. Fagan's ST12 77* churches).

The final role of this localised Christian legend owes itself to 'Bran the Blessed', who also travelled with his son, Caradog to Rome, and then returned to Wales, sometime in the early years of the first century CE. According to this legend, it was purported that Bran was the one who preached the Christian gospel to the people of the Vale of Glamorgan first, before Illtyd. Legend records Bran preaching at, of all places, Sully. Allegedly the Roman military had built a causeway over to the Sully Island at this time also. Naturally with these types of legends, it is debatable whether there was any point in building a causeway over to *Sully Island (ST16 66),* for there seems no particular reason, and there is limited artifactual evidence for Roman occupation at the location. And the reason for the legendary Bran to have preached at Sully in the first place is clearly a mystery. These Historians, where do they come up with these ideas?

There is clearly an obsession with linking early Christianity in the Roman period with the Vale of Glamorgan: we need to turn our attention to hard facts. There is mention of raids along the Vale of Glamorgan coast at existing monasteries or 'schools', possibly sited at the well established *Llancarfan (ST05 70)* and *Llantwit Major (SS96 68)* sites. These early religious sites were built in secluded valleys, but maybe in 520 ce these sites were located and looted. Later still these Vale of Glamorgan sites were renowned for the education of renowned saints such as: David, Samson of Dol, Paul Aurelian, Gildas, Tudwal, Baglan and Patrick. At least, even though Christianity may not have arrived with the family members of Caractacus, it can be said that it was well established in the Vale of Glamorgan as the prominent religion by the mid 500's CE, only a few generations after the Western Roman Empire had ceased to exist.

Turning back to archaeology textbook facts, excavations at the *Atlantic Trading Estate (ST13 67)* in the 1980's gave us a cornucopia of evidence that assisted us in understanding the change from pagan to Christian burial practice. The late Roman to post-medieval cemetery at the *Atlantic Trading Estate* was an intact snap shot in time that archaeologists rarely obtain; a continuity of undisturbed and unbroken facts. A cemetery linked to the *Atlantic Trading Estate* site possibly established through pilgrimages was discovered at different times whilst houses were being constructed at the turn of the 1900's around the early medieval chapel at *St. Baruc's chapel (ST11 66)* on Barry Island. These burials occasionally may have been late Roman, but the skeletal remains were not recorded methodically using archaeological standards.

Reports from the Second World War tell us that there was a lead coffin found close to the cemetery excavations at the *Atlantic Trading Estate (ST13 67)* in the 1980's, but little detail was recorded, the coffin being melted down for scrap. This was probably late Roman from the latter part of the 300's ce. The burial in this case was probably pagan. Some of the inhumation burials found at the cemetery were orientated with the head towards the north, interred by relatives from a nearby Roman settlement. Samples of Roman glass demonstrate that some of the pagan Romans were cremated, and ashes placed into glass jars (an example is on display in the Legionary Museum at

Caerleon (ST34 90). The later post-Roman Christian burials orientated the head towards the east and were interred by relatives of the deceased who had a desire to buried along a pilgrimage route, potentially leading to and from the Barry Island possible religious sites. Both pagan and Christian burial practices respected each other, traditions of inhumation continuing, but with rituals dedicated to a new god. Parts of the seaward cemetery area have been eroded by the sea over the centuries. Here the remaining cemetery is excavated in sand dunes around a well. The acid sandy soil here hasn't in places been adequate to preserve human bone, but those skeletal remains that have survived have been very revealing. The wooden coffins (probably made from shipwrecked timbers), clothing, and any body-wrapped shrouds would have decayed due to the higher acid content in the sand. But the archaeological evidence including gold rings (still in situ on the fingers of the burial), jewellery, and other artefacts have survived.

Many wells with a purported religious significance have been cited in the Vale of Glamorgan, some of which no doubt have their origin in the Roman period, others clearly not. These were likely to have been part of domestic living requirements in the main or for pilgrimage purposes; as going to the local pagan or Christian places of worship and dedication.

Early evidence for Christianity in Roman period Britain is very scant. It is in the period after the Roman occupation that Christianity leaves its mark. Evidence for pagan religion, is also limited in extent in the Vale of Glamorgan. But the legends are worth a mention, and with every legend, there may be some facts to be picked out here and there, hidden in the story telling and narrative history.

CHAPTER 4
THE ACTIVITIES OF LIFESTYLE, DEATH AND COMMUNICATION

Part 1 Settlements

This chapter will be devoted to the levels of Romanised settlement in the Vale of Glamorgan.

We place our attentions towards the isle of *Barry Island (ST11 66)*. Scant evidence has indicated a Romanised 'settlement' under the present day fun fair, with due attention given to the possible Roman well (now covered up) linking the two pieces of evidence, lying alongside the 'Romans' Well Road', a stone's throw from the railway bridge. John Storrie explored the area extensively, citing extensive medieval occupation in the area of the well and under the fun fair, but alongside this evidence Roman coins and pottery were excavated. A curiosity mentioned on maps of the late 1800's is the mention of an 'Ancient British Kitchen.' John Storrie excavated this location, coming to the learned conclusion that it was of Roman period occupation. A short distance away from Barry Island on the mainland, we can cite a Roman period partially- excavated farmstead beneath the ruins of the Medieval *Barry Castle (ST10 67)* and a further site which has been located at *Cold Knap (ST10 66)*.

It would be fitting to interject at this point with the extensive archaeological data from the excavation (1977–1979) at *Biglis (ST14 69)* that occupies a tump. Biglis is a large settlement with an extensive reach and command over the landscape, with access to a navigable Cadoxton River. This site made with its lower levels constructed from Lias limestone slabs (locally quarried), timber frame with wattle and daub panels to build up the height to the roof level, with a roof thatched utilising the local reeds harvested from the marsh land that surrounded the Cadoxton River, immediately to the South of the site. Roman pottery was excavated in abundance, with evidence of iron smelting from the samples of slag recorded, and numismatic evidence, such as three radiate coins from the late 200's, and a coin of Constantine II (336-340 CE). Other coins have been recovered post-excavation, but the vital information of their locations were not recorded and the items were sold on 'EBay' by treasure hunters, evidence lost. A Roman fibula brooch was also excavated. A positive assemblage of finds indicating the continuity of occupation, various activities, the iron processing alongside farming, and the link in the chain of the Roman Villa network, at one of *Ely (ST14 76)* Roman Villa's outlaying farmsteads. Close to the *Biglis (ST14 69)* site are the believed remains of a Roman farmstead site at Cassy Hill (ST13 69), that overlooks *Cadoxton Church (ST12 69)* and evidence in the form of pottery and building material for another farmstead has been indicated at *Palmerston (ST13 69)*.

Recent evidence by the author, picked up through field survey work with his students, from a ridge overlooking Porthkerry to the north indicates a farmstead here (known as *West Ridge ST08 67*). Re-used Roman Samian, mortaria, building material and other pottery has been located through field walking at West Ridge.

Dinas Powis Common (ST15 70) and the *Pop-Hill Dinas Powis (ST15 70)* farmstead sites have offered us more tantalising proof to the intensity of farming in the Vale of Glamorgan. Pop Hill has offered us building material and evidence for metal working (iron slag), as well as the usual pottery and, interestingly enough, a blue glass bead. Although these sites have offered us artifactual evidence, and the earthworks of the latter of the two sites is tantalising, these farmsteads are fairly modest. Nevertheless, they paint a refreshing picture of Romanisation of the landscape. Close to these Dinas Powis sites there is *Pen-y-lan Cardiff (ST19 78)* - another potential farmstead site that supplied the Roman Villa at *Ely (ST14 76)*.

Another potential farmstead site of note was located at the *Cosmeston Medieval Village (ST17 68)* excavations. Roman pottery and coinage was excavated, and a ditch connected to a farmstead type site was excavated running beneath the Cosmeston medieval stratification.

What we have in mind for the vicinity of the settlements in the western Vale particularly at *St. Donat's (SS93 68)* is based on speculation. Were the earlier reports of a Roman structure at St. Donat's based in any way on fact? We cannot be sure, but the findings over the years of over 30 Roman period coins in the St. Donat's vicinity, and a believed statue of Mercury, are definitely worth a note here.

Individual Roman coinage and hoards have been located throughout the landscape across the Vale of Glamorgan, and many items through trade from far away parts of the empire are also known from our Roman sites. Such artefacts indicate the ability of the local population to trade in a range of produce, both locally and far and wide.

There are signs of some of the earlier pre-Roman native hill-forts being re-occupied; if only on a modest limited scale. Those sites that we are lucky enough to have excavated evidence from are at *Llancarfan Castle Ditches (ST05 70), Victoria Park Barry (ST13 69)* and *The Bulwarks Porthkerry (ST08 66)*. These hill-forts offered ready-made protection against wild animals. The rich external and internal arrangements varied from site to site. Some of them had been deserted generations before at the time of the Roman control in the Vale of Glamorgan. These would have been re-utilised for cultivation and small-scale domesticated farmsteads; attached outposts to the villa network.

Potential Roman farmstead sites indicated through pottery finds exist at a variety of sites in the western Vale of Glamorgan, including a site near *Llanmihangel (SS98 71)*. It is here where hewn slabs and tiles have been found. Proven farmstead sites have been excavated and aerial-mapped at *Cae Summerhouse Tythegston (SS98 66)* which overlooks the sand dunes at Merthyr Mawr.

Larger scale vicus sites around military garrisons were established at *Cowbridge (Bovium SS99 74)*. A bathhouse, shops, and other structures have been excavated there. Structural evidence is lacking, but again a large-scale Roman site may exist to be discovered in the *Llysworney (SS96 74)* surrounds.

I have only touched upon a small number of sites and settlement centres in this section, but these and more are listed in this book under the heading *'Inventory of sites and non-coin finds.'*

Furthermore, to be believed or not, the architecture of the Roman landscape was reconstructed by Iolo Morgannwg (Edward Williams 1747 – 1826) the late 1790's Cowbridge historian. He claimed that there were two substantial Roman sites at *Llanmaes (SS98 69)*, near Cowbridge. He explained about one of these purported Roman sites as being Llantwit Major castle in a field called the Hays about 50 metres east of Bedford castle. He traced this potential Roman site, and fairly confusingly stated that it was on lower ground to the west side of Llanmaes brook were foundations were found, this is clearly not the medieval tower presently standing, named as Llanmaes castle, north east of Bedford castle. Iolo described that locals had reported to him that Roman statues, coins and other metal artefacts had been discovered (mind you, this was in a time that everything of any age, was deemed to be Roman). What type of site do these indicate: a settlement, Villa or even a temple? Although the *Caermead (SS95 69)* Roman Villa is less than a mile away from this potential Llanmaes Roman site location, it is unlikely to have been a Villa in close proximity to another. This potential site may now have been lost forever, covered by spoil from the Llantwit Major Road by-pass alongside other known archaeological sites.

An interesting story now follows, as one example of the type of reports we archaeologists receive; as highlighted for this publication, came to me when I was a student in the first year of comprehensive school in 1986. An inspirational teacher (Mr. Webber) informed me of a friend now passed on to the 'summerlands', whom he knew before going to a college at Caerleon. This friend lived at *Daniel Street Barry (ST12 69)*. He once showed him a very curiously shaped earthenware jar that had been found in his garden. The future teacher, thinking nothing of this, went on with his career. Years later he went back to see his friend with the news that the curiously shaped earthenware jar was a 'face jar' decorated with a Roman soldier, similar to one on display at the *Legionary Museum at Caerleon (ST34 90)*. Alas the wife of his friend had some unfortunate news; her husband had passed away only a few years before. On inquiring about the jug, the wife exclaimed, 'that horrible looking jug, I threw it out with the rubbish'. Horrified, there was nothing the old friend could do. In turn there were other reports of findings in the vicinity that linked in with the discovery of the 'face jug': blue glass beads in a black loamy earth mound had been discovered in the field at the top of *Daniel Street (ST12 69)*. Also to the rear of *Daniel Street* in the allotment earth, Roman coins have been allegedly found. Any settlement here has been completely developed on over the past 120 years.

The considerable number of potential Roman occupational sites in the Vale of Glamorgan, indicate a high degree of Roman development resources (military, administration and trade) being placed into the region. It is likely that many of the sites that have been urbanised in the Vale of Glamorgan since the medieval period are the same locations that would have been urbanised by the Romans. The concentration of Roman sites in the form of farmsteads and 'vici' in and around Barry, Cowbridge, Dinas Powis and even Llantwit Major is testament to the native urbanisation.

This focal point of occupation in the Vale of Glamorgan, enriched by its agricultural wealth, may have supported a population of around 20,000 people alongside a Roman military presence. At these figures it can be surmised that the complete population of Wales using modern boundaries in around the 100's CE, was around 200,000 people (native and settlers), and may have increased further as vici increased their size around the military bases they were supporting, and under the patronage and protection of the Roman military. Pax Romana brought the population of Britain relative peace, structure and settlement.

The ratio of native peoples and settlers in Wales supported a military garrison, of 16 to 1. These people were administered at the lowest level through the Villa network, and from there on up to the regional political capitals; the political units (civitas capitals). These were the political units of administration for the Romans.

Part 2 Villas and other settlements

The section will consider the role and nature of the Roman Villa network in the Vale of Glamorgan.

There are a number of different status types and size of Villa in the Vale of Glamorgan. Before the 1950's we only really knew about two of them, *Ely (ST14 76)* and *Caermead (SS95 69)*, but since then we have confirmation of more that have been excavated due to the development boom and through new discovery techniques (aerial photography, geophysics and so on). At the site of the *Ely (ST14 76)* Roman Villa first excavated by John Storrie in 1894, there have been various numismatic findings, such as Augustus 27 BCE - 14CE., Nerva 96-98 CE and Antoninus Pius 138-161 CE coin denominations, fairly early issues for a Roman Villa is the region. The Ely Roman Villa featured tessellated flooring, a bath house block with hypocaust system, and wall plaster in rooms. All this has been discovered through various seasons of excavations at the site, and indicates a high-status type villa with the luxury and wealth of an edge-of-empire villa, reminiscent of examples from south-central England. The site's major stone phase of construction dates to the 100's CE, and ceased in the early 300's CE. It has positive traces of iron smelting (the site of a foundry), taking advance of the rich seems of iron found at *Goldsland (ST10 71)* wood and *Rhiwbina (ST15 81)*. The archaeologist John Storrie, who first discovered and excavated the *Ely (ST14 76)* site, remarked to it being an extraordinary find. In John Storrie's excavations he located a silver denarius of *Antoninus Pius (138-161 CE)*, and bronze Quadrans of Augustus (27 BCE - 14CE), along with two other coins, a variety of metal objects, and a copious amount of pottery typical for such a site. On this excavation (one of many of his), plans of the structure including the bath block, and illustrations were made of the tessellated courtyard. In addition there were further discoveries of coins from usurper Emperor Carausius (287-93) and Emperor Constantine I (reign of 320 - 324). These showed that the site enjoyed a long period of occupation. The Ely Villa was once believed to be fairly unique, but since the discovery of particularly the *Langstone (ST38 89)* Roman Villa in 2001, the *Ely (ST14 76)* Villa is no longer so uniquely placed.

North West of the *Ely (ST14 76)* Villa in the late 1700's, Iolo Morgannwg (Edward Williams 10 March 1747 – 18 December 1826) purported to have discovered the site of a 'large' ancient 'bloomery' (smelting iron from its oxides), near the Ely bridge (mentioned as Lan-y-lai bridge). At this site some time before Iolo's time, there were many finds reported to have been discovered in a layer of 'cinder', and included pottery and coins. Most of these Roman finds were discovered in 1752 CE in the grounds of Lan-Ely hall, due west of our Villa but the exact find spot has not been located. This site, if it is not part of the Ely Roman Villa estate, may be an iron smelting site, which had ready access to the Iron ore mines at *Goldsland (ST10 71) wood, Miskin (ST06 84)* and *Rhiwbina (ST15 81)*.

The *Caermead Llantwit Major (SS95 69)* Roman Villa is also seen as utilising local iron deposits with evidence of iron smelting, which was discovered by John Storrie in 1887, and based on the account prepared by Iolo Morgannwg. It is also known as 'Gaermead', prospering in the 300's ce, as opposed to the earlier prosperity of the *Ely (ST14 76)* Roman Villa. It would have been exposed to the raids believed to have occurred on this stretch of the coast by pirates in the late 300's ce. Alas, it seems that the site succumbed to these raids sometime in the later 300's ce, as at least 37 of the people whose skeletal remains excavated at the site, found above a mosaic floor alongside 3 horse skeletons were, it seems, massacred. Some show signs of skull fracture, reminiscent of axe blows. The Caermead Roman Villa has a bath house block and a large courtyard with finds from the site including Pennant sandstone roofing tiles, painted wall-plaster, fragments of sculptured figures, window glass, and column fragments. Many varieties and type of pottery have been excavated at the site over the years as well as a number of Roman coins from a variety of Emperors', including Constantius II (337 - 361 CE), illustrating the later occupation at the site. 38 coins were discovered at the site in 1956. Iolo Morgannwg (are Iolo's accounts as really unreliable as some archaeologists now make out?) recorded that the Villa was called the 'Moors castle', situated in a field called 'Gare Mead', where there were walls, human bones and an inscribed stone. These were thought to have been an early Christian monastery before, but discounted when John Storrie proved the site was a Roman Villa.

In 1956 local archaeologist Howard Thomas discovered the Roman farmstead at *Moulton (ST07 69)*. The *Moulton* farmstead was found to have painted wall-plaster, pennant sandstone roofing slabs and a coin from Constans (333 - 337 CE); it may have been abandoned alongside the *Caermead Villa* and for similar reasons. There are no signs of sophistication, no bath house block or mosaic flooring, and were certainly a humble farmstead and not a villa.

The *Whitton Lodge (ST08 71)* farmstead situated alongside the modern Five Mile lane (between Barry and Bonvilston) may have been a Roman Villa; but in this publication I have classed it as a farmstead for the time being, it was discovered by local archaeologist Howard Thomas in 1956 CE, noticing that it had a rectangular outlay in which was enclosed a courtyard, around this were described ditches. The 1956 CE report led to a large scale excavation in the 1970's CE. Interesting finds of a granary, fragments of painted wall-plaster, bath house block, tessellated courtyard, large numbers of pottery fragments, tegular roman roof-tile type, a coin of emperor Galleries (253 - 268 C.E) and *'blue glass beads'*.

Dan-y-graig (SS84 98) near Porthcawl is also purported to be a Roman Villa. It certainly suggests villa status, when in 1850 a broken tile and lime mortar floor was found, known to the Romans as Opus Signinum alongside fragments of painted wall-plaster, a corn dryer, and an unusual collection of iron objects: a key, iron nails in still positioned in a wooden board, and the coin of an empress!

Llandough (ST16 73) Roman Villa with bath block house was extensively excavated in 1979 in advance of development works. Construction dates are believed to be around the 120 - 130's CE, occupying an earlier Iron Age site. It seems to have suddenly been abandoned in the middle 300's CE.

The major problem with the discovery of any Roman site is the general perception that any new Roman site must all be Roman Villas. This is simply not true. Indicators of possible villa sites have come from all corners of the Vale of Glamorgan, in the form of earthworks, building material (roof tile-Tegula, pilae and such like), pottery and other artefacts. All this evidence may indicate a variety of sites: a farmstead, pottery kiln, cultivation and so on.

Conceivably the name *villa* conjures up a Roman type site, but in reality villas were few and far between locally.

Part 3 Burials (inhumation and cremation)

Roman inhumation and cremational burial, individually (for example *Biglis* *(ST14 69)*, *Caermead (SS95 69)*, and *Glan-y-mor (ST09 66))* and or as part of cemeteries (for example *Atlantic Trading Estate (ST13 67)*, *Ewenny (SS91 77)* and *Llandough (ST16 73))* have been excavated at a variety of locations in the Vale of Glamorgan.

In the late 1980's, the *Atlantic Trading Estate (ST13 67)* was the location of a late Roman and Medieval cemetery, where 45 inhumation burials were excavated in situ alongside a well. There were indications of cremation burials also. The site may have been part of a cemetery for a local unidentified settlement, or it was a pilgrim's burial site, alongside a pilgrim route. The graves (some lined with wooden planks or stone) contained an array of artefacts; including gold rings, pottery and coins. The site preserved in the mainly sandy beds, the staining on the contexts of the rotting wood of coffins or grave side lining. It is common knowledge at the site that in the Second World War where American servicemen were stationed, a number of artefacts were reported. Whilst constructing the camp; working on the construction of storage buildings, the GI's found a number of 'ancient artefacts' in foundation trenches and whilst digging soil for sandbags. Intact green Glass bottles (olla) containing a 'grey matter' were retained by some GI's as an 'ancient memento of their tour of duty in Britain.' It is also likely that at the time a number of bottles would have been discarded or taken to be recycled. The 'grey matter' contained in these bottles was described as being emptied out, and said bottles filled with liquor! Some fragments of 'blue' glass were excavated alongside the burials, but this evidence was very inconclusive. These bottles may have been cremation jars, similar to an example on display at the Roman Legionary Museum at *Caerleon (ST34 90)*. A lead coffin has also been reported to have been found at the *Atlantic Trading Estate (ST13 67)*. This coffin had been described as having intricate external designs on it, those of shells similar to an excavated example found at Colchester many decades later. This coffin may have been one of several discovered at the Atlantic Trading Estate.

Most of the bodies excavated at the Atlantic Trading Estate showed signs of a very common modern ailment; the diagnosis was that the internments suffered from arthritis. This was probably due to the damp conditions at the potential settlement nearby, which would have been prone to flooding from the *Cadoxton River (ST12 67)*: which was further north over 2,000 years ago. The bodies were buried at a time when inhumation was fashionable for both pagans and early Christians in the later stages of the Roman period. Cremation had been an earlier practise in Roman Britain, and may explain the lack of bodies at the cemetery from the 100's and 200's CE. They were simply placed in glass jars at another location on the Atlantic Trading Estate, and the discoveries mentioned above at the time of the Second World War bare out this. Other burials located in the Second World War period, to the east of the Atlantic Trading Estate to the rear of the 'Police Houses', were formerly reported also in 1974. These were eight aligned stone tombs, which have not been located since. The Atlantic Trading Estate may have been an extensive Roman and Medieval Burial ground, serving an extensive community yet to be located.

Excavations adjacent to the church of *St. Dochdwy Llandough (ST16 73)* in 1994 revealed 1,026 burials, as part of a building development scheme. The inhumations range in date from the very late Roman period (samples of amphora, have given use this dating evidence) through to the 1100's or later.

The excavations at *Biglis (ST14 69)* were also very revealing. 13 inhumations were found in a 'multiple' grave, and were the result (as we have found at *Caermead (SS95 69))*, of some kind of conflict in the later stages of the Roman period, and the decline of the Villa sites. Blue glass beads were associated with these burials also.

Dating burials is particularly fraught with one major problem: burials by their very nature cut through earlier archaeological contexts. But discoveries of datable material such as 'diagnostic' rims and bases of pottery, coins or jewellery, assist us in giving a date for the inhumations.

Readers will notice the mention of occasional 'blue glass beads' found on excavations (*Biglis ST14 69*, *Daniel Street Barry ST12 69*, and *Pop-Hill Dinas Powis ST15 70* for example), associated with burials. The black friable mound which contained 'blue glass beads' found in the field at the end of *Daniel Street Barry (ST12 69)* may have been a burial mound. Looking for evidence outside the region, at *Coelbren (SN85 10)* and *Loughor (SS56 98)* Roman forts; similar beads have been excavated, except that they are more ornate with incised engraved lines, and they were found to be a lighter shade of blue. A '*blue glass bead*' was found at *High Pennard (SS54 88)* on the Gower.

At *Castle-upon-Alun St. Bride's Major (SS91 74),* workmen unearthed three inhumations dating back to the early stages of the Roman Period. The burials contained native occupants, indicated by iron spear heads, daggers and other items. These burials may relate to a period of conflict, or may simply be the standard burial practice of natives at the time. At the *Old Castle Down (SS90 75)* above St. Bride's Major, there is evidence to point towards a considerable conflict, with the defender's vigorous controlling of the ridge here, as indicated through the burials from the early Roman period. Or is this a simple case of misinterpretation.

Single burials and small groups of burials are present on several Roman Villa sites: *Llandough (ST16 73)*, and *Caermead (SS95 69* Other than the 37 victim bodies of the 'massacre' excavated at Caermead, there were 6 formal burials excavated also). The vicus at *Cowbridge Bovium (SS99 74)* has given us tantalising burial evidence, with one excavated body, and on the western outskirts of the settlement there was excavated the ornamentally carved lion of Cowbridge; originally one of 4 finials that capped the corners of a senior military or administrators tomb. Roman period burials have also been excavated at the site of the *Ewenny Priory (SS91 77)* along with pottery for dating evidence. A burial from *Llangan (SS96 77)*, two from *Merthyr Mawr (SS85 77)*, a further one from *Llantwit Major (SS96 68)* and *Newton Porthcawl (SS84 77)* are believed to date from the Roman period. Excavated cemeteries or single burials would have indicated little of the racial make-up of their incumbents. After the 100's ce the population burials would have been practically impossible to differentiate the racial make-up, representing the diverse cosmopolitan Roman Empire. For instance, a black Roman Legionary, Arab trader or native all living and dying alongside each other. Coinage and jewellery such as Roman Fibulae brooches are also associated with burials.

The burials and cremations mentioned here only represent a small sample number of human remains excavated in the region from the Roman period. Those yet to be discovered will give us a further insight into the health and age of the population, and how they died (natural, warfare or something more sinister as at Caermead) *(SS95 69)*.

Part 4 Wells and Springs

In this part, I am going to write about the Roman wells and springs in the Vale of Glamorgan. There are many natural water sources that have been bastardised and exploited in the Roman period and continued in use, in some cases into modern times. Stone wells were not really constructed in the Iron Age; the Roman examples are the first stone built wells.

The most notable well in this publication is the *'Roman Well', Romans Well Road (ST11 66)* on Barry Island. This is a substantial structure; when it was used its aperture was 2ft 6 inches in diameter and the walls were 4ft 9inches in diameter. The well was first recorded by John Storrie, where he also identified Roman pottery, and other items from a variety of periods. He also found another assemblage of Roman material nearby which was found at a medieval settlement, given the name of 'Peirio's Abbey' by the 1530's chronicler John Leland. There is no doubt that the well standing at present was used by a Medieval community, but may well have been constructed in the Roman period, to service the needs of a potential *vicus* nearby. Also at St. Barruc's chapel, also re-discovered by John Storrie at the same time period, Roman pottery and two coins were excavated. Was the well used as part of the late Roman, Christian or pagan pilgrimage route on the Barry Island? The local Lias Limestone masonry used in the construction of the well was similar in construction to Roman examples elsewhere. The well has not been destroyed, and when it is uncovered again, we can re-examine it, and make an educated guess as to its origins.

There are 'wells' recorded and marked on maps as 'Roman Wells' located in the Vale of Glamorgan. Whether these are Roman in origin to the truest extent, is debatable. Some 'well' examples have been located close to existing known Roman sites. One such example, *(SS08 66)* is more of a spring and is found alongside the *Bullhouse Well (ST07 67)*. These are close to the re-used Iron-Age defences at *The Bulwarks (ST08 66)*, and *West Ridge (ST08 67)* Roman farmstead at Porthkerry.

At *Pencoetre Barry (ST12 70)* there have been several recording and spurious sightings made over the years about so called Roman wells there. Alongside one of the well sites, a Roman corn-drying kiln was remarked upon. Potential Wells that may have been constructed in the Roman period exist at *Peters Well Road Barry (ST10 68)*, and *Porthkerry (ST07 67)*. Recorded close to the *Glan-y-mor 'Official Building' (ST09 66)*, a potential Roman well was remarked upon. But as with anything discovered over the centuries and marked down on maps by a surveyor or cartographer, everything was deemed to be of Roman origin.

We have looked at a scant few examples of wells in the Barry area, we simply cannot examine every case of a well in the Vale of Glamorgan, they are just too numerous. The task is endless. Eight locations for example marked on the modern 151 Ordnance Survey map as springs or wells immediately in and around *Llantwit Major (SS96 68)*, and a further potential site known as *Peterswell House (ST96 70)*. Other springs and wells in such a limited sample area are also indicated elsewhere. Let us say that in the Roman period, people needed to drink and that some of the 'wells and springs' mentioned here were definitely used and constructed. Well shafts were excavated and masonry applied for the first time at this Roman period.

Part 5 Roman Roads and trackways

It is fitting to discuss those route ways in the Vale of Glamorgan that have been given the grand title of a Roman road over the many centuries. Few of these roads, can only be described as nothing more than un-metalled track ways, or drovers paths that have as much to do with the Roman period as a modern Mobile phone. But some Roman roads are in fact that, they must have been! Usually the Roman roads were never straight, turning to deviate around water courses, natural earthworks and the like, following ridges. The *Via Julia Maritima* was in the main fairly straight.

What is known about this route? Now referred to as the A48 or as the 'Portway' ridge in the Vale of Glamorgan, between Bridgend via Cowbridge and Cardiff, is commanded by a natural ridge. This high ground of Carboniferous and Lias limestone (at some places 130 metres above sea level) is a vantage point which would have been a vital surveying indicator for a 'Roman road planner'. This route was originally metalled by the advancing Roman military in around the 50 to 70's CE. It offered the Romans a communication access to extend their network of roads to link the fort at *Cardiff (ST18 76)* with the fort and vicus at *Bovium Cowbridge (SS9974)*, and then onto the fort at *Nidvm (SS74 97)*, the Roman Neath. The most significant extent of the *'Via Julia Maritima'* road is to be found as a 'structural' trace as a Roman Agger at *St. Hilary (ST 01 73)*. The rest of the route is substantially slighted by the modern alignment of the A48 between *Cardiff (ST18 76)* and *Laleston (SS86 79)*. At *St. Hilary (ST 01 73)* the Agger is illustrated by a slight raised embankment along its south-east bounds heading out as a fork from the main A48 as it continues west-bound. The camber of the road at St. Hilary itself is highlighted and enclosed to the south by a shallow bank, and by a ditch more than 1 metre deep running along a stretch of the road, with a raised bank on the north as a curb. Moreover, the early 1800's ce 'road marker' towards 'The Clump' at St. Hilary, on the top of this route way, is the best indication that the road was still a main thoroughfare 1,700 years after it had been established by the

Romans. Historians through the years have stated that some of the artery roads leading to and from the A48 have Roman origin, but nothing has substantiated any of this.

The myth that Roman roads were all perfectly straight, in many cases is just that; the feeling is that the network of Roman road engineers had to sight their roads along ridges along the best and quickest alignment, many of these routes were far from being straight. However this is not a myth when you look at a majority of the stretch of road between *Cardiff (ST18 76)* and *Laleston (SS86 79)* that was the *Via Julia Maritima*, the Roman road is straight. A straight length of road is born out for the alignment between St. Hilary Down *(ST 01 73)* to *Stormy Down (SS84 80)* and *Heol-y-Sheet (SS83 80)* an approximate distance of some 12 miles. You may sight today, driving east bound from Bridgend along the modern A48, heading out of *Pentre Meyrick (SS96 75)*, a straight alignment. This slightly disappears just after Cowbridge, but is suddenly perfectly highlighted by an avenue of trees of the *St. Hilary Down (ST00 74)*, ending in sight at 'The Clump' 130 metres above ordnance Datum. The *Via Julia Maritima* is traceable for lengths along the modern A48 alignment, and followed through some modern farm field boundaries at *Glanwenny (SS90 78)* and heading towards the *Redhill Laleston (SS86 79)* roundabout.

The alignment of hedges, before the *Redhill Laleston Roundabout*, with a command to the south, leading off from the A48 west bound at *Laleston (SS87 79)* gives us tantalising evidence of a road surface. Heading in alignment towards the Redhill Laleston Roundabout in places, the hedge boundary crowns a metalled surface *(SS86 79)*, as discovered and recorded with my students on a field workshop in 2010. The Roman road surface along the latter hedge alignment retains a slight camber, and a concentration of field worn stones, standing out starkly and distinctly to the ploughed field's occasional Lias limestone regolith spread. Other curious sunken track alignments are also present in an easterly direction from the latter. This section of road close to the surface topsoil was revealed by recent cultivation, and left un-covered.

The section of *Via Julia Maritima* as referred to in the *Antonine Itinerary* (*Antonini Itinerarium*, a contemporary Roman document that registers road distances throughout the empire, of unknown date) easterly to *Cardiff (ST18 76)* from *Bovium Cowbridge (SS99 74)*, is traceable as straight ridgeway units under parts of the modern alignment of the A48, via *Bonvilston (ST08 74)*, with a useful Bronze Age Standing Stone marker, aligned along the route near to St. Nicholas. There are indicators as a 'sunken muddy track now colonised by mainly native trees' at a length of deteriorated road at '*The Downs*' *Culverhouse cross (ST11 74)*, long since bereft of use, but intriguing that it is on the *Via Julia Maritima* alignment. This muddy track may have been abandoned in antiquity, as borne out at 'the Downs', and was replaced by another road running immediately parallel to its north, now a raised partially metalled track highlighted by hedging; later abandoned for the modern diversion at the 'Tumbledown'.

However, what the historians don't tell you at school is that when the road network was constructed by the military, as they were the only units of engineers and manpower that were available to construct such works, that the maintenance was left in demilitarised zones to the 'vicus' civilian administrators and 'civitas capital' magistrates. As we have found, their maintenance was not a priority, and after just a few decades most of the Roman road network would have been severely potholed. In places it would have been so badly deteriorated that it was nothing more than muddy country tracks. The same thing happens today.

There is a field crop mark indicated through aerial photography, running south east in a trajectory from the existing Roman road at the top of *St. Hilary Down (ST01 73)*, this needs to be investigated.

It is more than likely that by 150 CE, the *Via Julia Maritima* resembled a country track, with much of the metalled surface worn down, or having slipped into the now silted up drainage ditch alongside it.

More probably spurious Roman roads have been sighted at *Candleston (SS86 77)* sand dunes, and near the *Llancarfan Castle Ditches (ST05 70)*. Certainly the report from the latter runs along a ridge. But there is no hard evidence with many of these reports to go by. The same can be said for any legendary road alignments in the Llantwit Major, St. Athan and Penllyn areas. These may follow natural ridge ways, but did the Roman military really have the time and stomach to build all these roads, without the modern equipment we use today, and for what purpose? Paved or metalled roads, as archaeologists have discovered, were not always the best ways of marking a route for 'traffic.' Sometimes these route ways were marked by simple standing stones or 'milestones' erected as markers, but there would have always been a surface of some description (this stands to reason). As discovered at Aberavon, Margam and Pyle (on display at the *Margam Stones Museum SS 80 86*, see *Gazetteer of visible Roman remains...*). Some standing stones already existed from pre- Roman times, on the ridgeways - the instant marked track ways of the day. Intriguing too is the Bronze Age standing stone at *St. Nicholas (ST08 74)*, which just happens to be on the *Via Julius Maritima* alignment. Rarely have we distances marked on the stones or the military unit who had erected the memorial but in places they do exist. At Pyle in 1835 an auxiliary unit erected a standing stone purportedly alongside the Roman road alignment (now on display at the *Swansea Museum SS65 92)* probably close to Pyle (as the stone had clearly been resighted at its 1835 erection spot). The inscription reads: IMP C M C PIAVONIO VICTORINO AUG translated as: for the Emperor Caesar Marcus Piavvonius Victorinus Augustus, who reigned as the Gallic Usurper between 269 - 270 CE. Better still we find a potential stretch of Roman road with a 'milestone' (inscribed IMP C M C L POSTVMO AVG G) alongside each other, with a carved dedication to the stretches rebuilding, with a date given by the emperor Caesar Marcus Cassianius Latinius Postumus Augustus as between 259 - 268 CE at

Melincryddan Neath (SS74 96), this stone is now displayed at the *National Museum and Galleries of Wales (ST18 76*, see *Gazetteer of visible Roman remains...)*. Both the Victorinus and Postumus stones were probably constructed by a detachment of auxiliaries from the same unit, heading out from a west Wales location, repairing the Pyle section last.

Such markers used as sign posts were sometimes nothing more than a stone dragged from the adjacent field; the field scatter of glacial erratic stone left over from the Devensian glaciation 12,000 years or more before, that were then erected along the alignment. Such a potential stone may be found at the *Sarn Helen (SN88 11)* as noted by the author and his students.

There is an interesting local legend at Aberthaw and the only ghost story in this book: it's a bit of fun. Along the stretch of road leading into Aberthaw from Rhoose (which is fairly aligned), a headless skeleton was found alongside the early foundations of a road, believed to be Roman. For some years a headless Roman soldier ghost was seen walking across the road, with it seems the lower part of his legs walking below the road surface. Then on extending the boundaries of the road, a 'skull' was found. Both head and body were re-united, and the ghost was never seen again. The ghostly aberration it seems had been looking for his head (The academics will love this mention in the book, I can't wait for the criticism, frankly I've gone past caring).

All the evidence for true Roman roads is limited to the *Via Julia Maritima* in the Vale of Glamorgan, although the amount of information for projected or assumed Roman roads would extend this section several times over. The basic rule to follow in regards to a potential Roman road is that they follow and occupy high ground, and the re-use of native track ways in the Roman period taking a variety of routes cannot be discounted either, as people would have had to travel from point A to point B. Modern roads that follow Roman roads, alas, destroy all signs of the early incumbent. Generally, people are obsessed with the fact that Roman roads are everywhere, the real fact is they are NOT. But nevertheless it is a cultural time-signature to the Roman legacy wherever one is found.

Roman roads simply fell out of use, as do modern roads after a short period of time, if not maintained. You only have to leave a modern narrow single carriage country road (the same width as the average Roman road); 5 years before water furrows out the centre of the road, the hedge colonises and grows out of control, and basically the road becomes nothing more than a depression. Roman roads unless maintained by its military builders and patrons on a yearly basis, became dirt tracks rapidly. The use of rivers and streams by the local population became far more attractive than the muddy road ways. Few roads were ever constructed by the Romans locally or elsewhere in Wales for that matter, in light of all this.

Let's get away from the road theory and move to something more tangible transportation possibilities. In Norfolk, for example, in light of the sea level being up to 5 metres higher than it is today, the Romans canalised (straightened and widened) existing water sources. Many rivers here would have been used in this way, as access by river to a number of our inland sites is more feasible this way.

Chapter 5
Fortifications

In the Vale of Glamorgan there were many Roman fortifications built for a military purpose, but some were re-used Iron Age hill forts. This can be determined through archaeological evidence, cartographical, hearsay, or historically indicated. These Roman military works are described as 'practice works or camps, marching camps', forts, fortlets or even re-used Iron-Age sites. It is quite fitting to state that with some of the Roman military wares such as Black Burnished ware being excavated at some Iron Age hill-forts that these were re-used temporarily by Roman garrisons. For example at *Blaen-cwm Bach (SS79 98)* a Roman military works was located at the partially surviving and then recently utilised Iron Age hill-fort. Then domestication occurred at some of these sites, as seen with the excavated evidence at *Castle Ditches Llancarfan (ST05 70)*, with the discovery of pottery and associated human bones.

Indications of Roman occupation are offered to us at the *Castle Ditches Llantwit Major (SS96 67)* hill-fort, where a considerable hoard of Carausius coins has been found. Local legend has it that these defences commanding the Colhugh natural harbour, accommodated the 'Roman troops' before they departed for the last time in the early 400's CE (I will never live this down mentioning this again).

Other reused hill-forts are indicated at *Caer Dynnaf Cowbridge (SS98 74)*. Discoveries of Roman pottery and quern stones from a contemporary structure indicate the sites re-use as a farmstead, after a Roman military use maybe. At *Cae Summerhouse Llantwit Major (SS99 66)* hill-fort, is a further example of re-use in the Roman period, where pottery has also been located. East of the *Llantrithyd House (ST03 73)*, a native farmstead or univallate hill-fort, prior to the Roman period continued in use, more probably just as a domesticated site indicated by the Roman pottery and a rotary quern excavated here also.

We have extensive evidence for the re-use of other tribal hill-forts in other parts of 'Glamorgan', such as *High Pennard (SS56 86)* on the Gower, where Roman period material has been located including a fragment of mortaria, and at *Hen Dre'r Gelli Rhondda (SS97 94)*, a native farmstead has offered us Roman pottery also.

Now a look at each individual Roman military work in brief.

The standard Roman military works of the first century were garrisoned by around 500 to a 1,000 personnel (Full unit). Auxiliaries consisting mainly of foot infantry, but in some locations up to one quarter of the unit's strength, were cavalry as at *Y Gaer Breconshire (SO00 29)*. The occasional garrison was primarily made up of auxiliary cavalry with a Roman officer in charge. In Wales the history of some of the fortlets is very obscure, mainly due to the fact that a number of active units were withdrawn in the mid 100's to build and maintain the frontiers works at the Antonine and Hadrian Walls, offering us limited occupation evidence. The following is an educated list of how many active forts were occupied throughout Wales from around 80 ce to 330 CE, and also of the status for *Cardiff Castle (ST18 76)* Roman fort occupation

Year all in CE fort	Number of permanent military sites in Wales	Status of Cardiff Castle
80	32	Full unit
110	31	Half unit
130	21	A holding detachment
150	19	A holding detachment
170	14	A holding detachment
190	12	A holding detachment
220	11	A holding detachment
293	Re-garrisoned sites in Wales	Possibly a Full unit
330	10	Full unit

Despite the lack of a combat garrison at Cardiff between 130 - 220 CE, 'A Holding Detachment', an administrative maintenance unit continued at the fort, no more than centuriae strength. However, occasionally extra to the 'Holding Detachment'; a *centuria* (a century of around 80 auxiliary soldiers with roman centurion and officers) may have been stationed at the fort between 130 - 220 CE, to assist with some defensive coastal activities along the coast.

The Cardiff Castle Roman Fort was rebuilt at least four times, every time enlarging or changing its boundaries. The fort at Cardiff was set out in the standardised Roman fashion, similar to the Legionary fortress at Caerleon but five times smaller. The complete eastern wall in its final phase, and over half of the south and north walls, have been used as foundations for the romantic rebuild that emulated the castle in the later decades of the 1800's CE. This western shore forts final phase base template, the original Roman wall foundations up to 2 metres high have been outlined in local red Radyr sandstone, visible to us today. Excavations have been extensively undertaken at this site, as recent as 2005. Roman building material, pottery and the other detritus of Roman occupation has been excavated. These most formidable defences offered the local population, who lived at the vicus that surrounded the fort and serviced its harbour, the protection needed at times of trauma.

There are two main locations for stone built military sites here, the most substantive as discussed above, and the other we turn to now is *Cowbridge (SS99 74)*. The argument against *Cowbridge* not being a fort is very weak. It is certain that a garrison of an unknown size was eventually superseded by a civilian vicus, as with the case at many other Roman forts. We do know from the archaeological evidence over the past three decades that stone built structures, defences, and numerous artefacts have been located. Military style baths at the Arthur John Car park site of the shops alongside the modern High Street and other structures have been excavated. Alongside the usual artefact assemblage for a Roman site, a tile stamped with the mark of the second Augustus Legion and beautiful sandstone carved lion, are all hallmarks of a military garrison.

It is more likely than ever that the legendary site of *Bomium (Bovium)* that was referred to in the *Antonine Itinerary (Antonini Itinerarium*, a contemporary Roman document that registers road distances throughout the empire, of unknown date) is that very site that we have referred to above as the fort at *Cowbridge*. Even the very first part of the name 'Bov', must indicate that it refers to the Latin word Bovine for Cow, the etymology, derives this from Latin genus 'bos' for the aurochs or ox and domestic cattle, and then later to Bovini. With the long field research of a Bridgend lad, Doug M. Jones, and two publications later from the mid 1980's (Search for (undated) *Bomium Field Work of a Local Archaeologist* and (undated) *Bomium A local History of Bridgend and surrounding Villages, searching throughout the bounds of the County of Bridgend and western Vale of Glamorgan*), he found nothing substantive, alas to say that *Bovium* was anywhere else other than *Cowbridge*. But he was certain that a substantive Roman site was to be found under the template of the Medieval Priory, or close by. The enigma of the Roman fort of *Bovium*, alas not at *Cowbridge* (when all the evidence is there) in the Ewenny area is continuous and relentless, and furthermore, what of a

Roman fort at *Kenfig*? But let's agree that *Cowbridge* is *Bovium (Bomium)*, the facts are clear.

Legend has it that there are military works in the locality or surrounds of the medieval castle at *Kenfig (SS80 82)*, and going by the place name evidence: *Old Castle Down (SS90 75)*, St. Brides Major and the commanding typography around Ewenny indicate further Roman military works alongside various locations of contemporary pottery and other material. Speculation leads us to an enclosure surrounded by linear earthworks a stones-throw west from *Ogmore Castle (SS88 76)*, it was reported that 'Roman parade helmet and contemporary pottery was located'. The author has excavated this site with his students, with no resultant discoveries of Roman date. Sites of military works are projected at a number of other locations. However, field work has revealed no fresh evidence at these locations either. Roman pottery has also been found at the location of *Candleston Castle (SS87 77)*, potentially the medieval fortifications were based on Roman earthworks? *Cefn Hirgoed (SS92 82)* is where we turn for actual Roman earthworks of one set, more probably two sets of defences for marching camps, one set having been destroyed by the motorway.

Some of the Roman 'Marching and Practice camps' were established to protect the garrison for short periods of time against potential hostile action. Also they were established for raw recruits learning construction techniques, protecting main road links under construction, routes of communication, and commanding positions. But the main point here is the very nature of these types of camps is that they are temporary. This building work would have declined after the majority of garrisons were removed for the campaigning in Scotland from 110 ce onwards.

Where we go from here now is to conclude, that the number of military works available to us through archaeology and local legend in the Vale of Glamorgan have been mentioned here. And to expand on this I hope the publication: ***The inventory of sites and non-coin finds*** assists the reader.

CHAPTER 6
THE BRITISH EMPIRE OF CARAUSIUS AND ALLECTUS
(286 TO 296 CE)

Part 1 Carausius

This chapter will deal with Carausius; a usurper Roman Emperor, as no publication on the Romans is complete without a look at an individual Emperor, and in our case, why not a British one, with links to the local region through his notable hoards of coins, and the rebuild in his reign of the *'Official Building'* at the *Glan-y-mor (STO9 66)*.

So it is fitting now that we shall turn to Marcus Aurelius Mausaeus Carausius. He was born presumably sometime in the 240's ce in the Netherlands. It is believed that through hard work and determination he eventually reached the heady heights as commander of the British fleet *(The Squadron of the Classis Britannica)*, a very senior and prominent position at the time. We have little evidence as to when he was given this distinction. It is the case, however, that his promotion through the ranks at sea from a low rank auxiliary would have occurred through the 260 and 270's CE. He was tasked as a commander to project Roman control of the seas and coast around Britain and the northern Roman European coastline. The aim was to augment the defence of the coast with fresh defences. Carausius would not only have had control of the fleet along the British Province coastline, but a significant number of highly trained and motivated land based marines. He established new locations for defence such as harbours, signals stations and forts. He also improved the existing fort network along the coast known as *'the Saxon shore fort coast'* or as the *'Duke of the Saxon shore'*. He also probably restored the principal road network at the northern frontier. The effectiveness of this defence stratagem repelled the attackers from the 'East

English coastline' (this is about the time the '*Saxoni* (Saxon)' by name were first mentioned in literary records)

Britain was under weak central Roman leadership, and an Empire weakened by secessionist rulership in various provinces with various states (Gallic Empire 259 – late 273 CE, Palmyrene Empire summer 271 – 272 CE) breaking away from central rulership. Carausius took advantage of this situation with the earlier period of instability, and in late 286 CE he left the navy and proclaimed himself Emperor of Britain and some of the Northern provinces. However some historians believe that Carausius had been accused by the centralised government in 286 CE of an abuse of his power and condemned to death; and even profiteering from his military campaigns, without offering the tribute to the centralised authority. With all this Carausius broke away from central authority to save his own life, but he nevertheless was believed to be a very powerful leader of men.

His early life had been spent with the Menapian tribe of the Netherlands where he learnt his trade on a local merchant ship. He therefore understood what it meant to be independent from the centralisation of Rome. After 250 years of Roman rule, to many Britons, an independent organised Britain may have been an attractive prospect. The people of Gaul had longed to be free from the yoke of Roman rule. They had offered great resistance, as borne out by the campaigns of Gaius Julius Caesar (58 BCE to 51 BCE). With renewed hope the Gauls may have turned their support to the new usurper Emperor Carausius, believing that he may offer an autonomous civilised rule away from that of Rome. Carausius devised a new monetary system and minted at Camulodunum (Colchester), Londinium (London) and Rotomagus (Rouen, France). This consisted of a great deal of gold coinage which was very similar in terms of weight to that minted in Rome. One issue of coins represented Carausius, and the Roman Emperors' (Diocletian 284 – 305 CE and Maximianus I 286-310 CE, to portray unity of the Roman states, and his legitimacy.

Part 2 British Empire and Allectus

Usurper Emperor Carausius built a large fleet of small but fast combat ready ships. These became known as 'the Squadron of the Classis Britannica'. The fleet patrolled the whole coastline of Britain with the help of many signal stations along the coastline which guided the fleets towards enemy vessels. As it was very difficult to see attacking vessels at night, the construction of 'signal stations, and light houses' assisted the 100-strong fleet in locating enemy shipping. This gave it a great advantage, through communication and through lighting the waterways at set locations. One 'beacon' would show for miles around, especially against a landscape with little lighting. This beacon would reflect off any object sailing, or better still in areas such as the Severn estuary (See, *Chapter 2 the changing face of our coastline under Roman rule Part 5 Harbours*), where two beacons on opposing sides of the channel in line with each other, a pirate ship would break the beam; then with the light broken the pirate ship would therefore be detected, and investigated by a patrol.

Usurper emperor Carausius was entrusted with the future of Britain and other formerly centrally-controlled Roman north-European provinces. The fresh approach of Carausius over this newly divided Roman Empire was for this smaller unit to support itself as an autonomous state from Rome. It was to provide for its own needs without supplying tribute to the distant centrally-controlled empire. The loyalty of a military force around Carausius would seem sufficient to add stability to this new found usurper empire. As an army of defence, it was an organised force, with a powerful efficient navy.

The first action of usurper emperor Carausius was to ensure the lowlands of Gaul were secure. He used a command of respect that was offered by his auxiliary and legionary forces there to achieve this aim. Supported by his naval supremacy, his fleet could act with readiness for emergencies.

Carausius was suitably confident in his hold on his new empire. He issued the legendary 'three headed coin', portraying himself, and the other two Emperors' in control of the empire (*see above*). This had so enraged the legitimate Emperors', as the coin had portrayed Carausius as legitimate in his hold of the northern Roman provinces, which was simply not the case.

Allectus, a loyal servant of usurper emperor Carausius had become one his senior officers. In seizing power in 286 CE, Carausius as ruler in utter defiance of Rome promoted Allectus to second in command, sometimes referred to as a Finance Minister. He travelled the country gaining support for the government of Carausius. At the same time he followed further orders to secure the coastline of Britain, to this aim supervising the construction of new forts and strengthening existing ones. He built and prepared military installations to prepare for any invasion from the north by Caledonian tribes, those from Ireland, and to repel the threat from the Saxoni raids on the south and east coasts of Britain.

Allectus acted as a powerful ambassador to usurper emperor Carausius in keeping with the spirit of *'Pax Romana'* across the British landscape. This would have nourished the relationship between Carausius and built up a level of trust. But for Carausius he would be sadly deceived, as all along Allectus had plotted to overthrow Carausius.

Usurper emperor Carausius and his minister Allectus may have visited the Vale to inspect the new building work at *Cardiff (ST18 76)*, which was to fortify against the increasing pressure placed onto Britain by attacks from foreign bodies. Carausius needed harbours for his navy and to supply his military on both sides of the English Channel. Carausius may have perceived the strategic properties of the *Porthkerry (ST08 66), Cold knap (ST10 66)* and *Old Harbour (ST08 66)* areas for supplies, installing further mooring posts and strengthening defences in these areas. The *Glan-y-mor 'Official building' (ST09 66)* was rebuilt at this period, as at this time it seems to have had official connections, probably for the military. It may have fallen into disrepair or been abandoned under the reign of the new usurper emperor Allectus, and was later demolished by the order of the future Roman Emperor Constantius (Chlorus) I.

Despite the agreeable relationship between Allectus and usurper Emperor Carausius, Allectus was unhappy and in 293 or 294 CE, motivated partly by greed, Allectus assassinated the usurper Emperor Carausius in Londinium (London), seizing power for himself. Unfortunately for usurper Emperor Allectus this proved to be a serious misjudgement for the future of the fledgling northern European independent Roman Empire. Allectus became a very unpopular leader and consequently the whole of Britain suffered.

Part 3 Allectus and the collapse of the Empire

Usurper Emperor Allectus it is alleged to have made a lot of expensive mistakes once he became the new emperor. Firstly, because of Allectus, many of the Roman officers he stationed in Britain were inexperienced and it became evident that they were young and poorly trained by Roman standards. In some cases it was noted that they could not properly manage the organisation and daily running of the trained legionary troops under their control. Allectus himself, who had previously been (it is suspected) a Finance Minister, was renowned for his lack of organisational ability and ineffective organisation of campaign armies. This was in stark contrast to his former boss Carausius, who had officers that had been consequently trained by Roman officers in the fleet and on land, and usually managed to get the best performance from his auxiliaries, legionaries and marines in battle.

The former usurper Emperor Carausius had the full support of his legions and their auxiliaries and other troops that had been used in successful campaigns in Gaul. Usurper Emperor Allectus wrongly believed he had the support of the auxiliaries based at Hadrian's Wall in his bid to protect Britannia from the Roman Emperors', the Saxoni and the other Germanic raiders.

Between 294 and 296 CE, in an attempt to win the war against Rome, the usurper Emperor Allectus withdrew all his remaining troops on the northern frontier of Britain, leaving it open to any attack from the north and any invasion on the Welsh coast. However, Allectus was still not sufficiently confident to leave the Saxoni shore undefended. He almost certainly gave incentives to Roman officers, so that they would fight for him, although collapse under Allectus became slowly apparent.

Two decades before the usurpation of Britain from centralised Roman control, there had been a number of provinces seceding from the Roman Empire, however one by one, the secessionists had been appeased by the sword and had re-entered the imperial yoke. An internal war with the Palmyrene Empire (summer 271–272 CE) ended in the east before 272 CE, and the re-absorption of the usurping Gallic Empire (259–late 273 CE). However, the Romans were left with the one remaining problem of instability within its borders by 287 CE. This was the newly established secessionist state of Britain. The future Roman Emperor Constantius (Chlorus) started to organise his forces to make concentrated attacks on the usurper Empire of Britain.

In 293 CE, Bolougne in Northern Gaul was captured by Roman forces. Boulogne was the main depot of the British Empire fleet, and had many ships open to capture in its harbour. Now there was a clear inability to defend the remaining secessionists' holdings in Gaul against the future Roman Emperor Constantius (Chlorus), making way for the last objective of Constantius: the invasion of Britain. By 296 CE Constantius had obliterated the majority of the remaining continental army strength of usurper Emperor Allectus in Gaul, and the transfer of Constantius's forces into Britain could begin in earnest (although some of the troops of Allectus remained un-checked for a short time).

Usurper Emperor Allectus's problems were exacerbated by the continuing problems along the northern British frontier, and along the West British coast. It is believed that in 296 CE, a full scale invasion had been led through breaches of unmanned posts at Hadrian's Wall. In other garrisoned locations little resistance was given by the few remaining Roman troops there. They succumbed to the vast enemy numbers, comprising a combined Pictish and Caledonian force. Open rebellion and civil war was believed to be occurring across Britannia also, between those forces loyal to Allectus, and those Roman and native aristocrat-led units allied to future Roman emperor Constantius (Chlorus) I and the co-Emperors' Diocletian and Maximianus.

Another occurrence was that the insecurity was causing the people of the Vale of Glamorgan to hide their precious goods and coin hoards, to prevent them falling into the hands of rogue elements. Unfortunately there was no effective administration across vast areas of Britain. Limited military garrisons offered little protection and barely upheld law and order. The people felt insecure and reacted to save what they had. The whole country was in a state of chaos. Consequently gold coins were being hidden in great hoards and in some cases the people who buried them would never return (*Colhugh Hill-fort SS96 67* and *Sully Moors ST14 68*). These hoards would be found by archaeologists centuries later. Newly constructed military buildings across Britannia, once planned by the former usurper Emperor Carausius to defend his new founded Empire, were left unfinished by usurper Emperor Allectus. The morale of the military deteriorated as by 296 CE Allectus was very unpopular. The east Britannia coast, once well protected by Carausius, was now open to attack. But when Allectus concentrated his efforts in the east with the surviving elements of '*The Squadron of the Classis Britannica*', the west coast was vulnerable to attacks as it lacked the naval patrols which were once successful under Carausius).

Usurper Emperor Allectus was now finding that he was not capable of running the whole country as well as his former boss Carausius had. The end of his reign in Britain was inevitable; it was just a question of when it would happen, rather than how. In the meanwhile, Allectus was forced to reorganise his military and administration in Britain. He moved the administration of the country to the Colonia Eboracensivm (York), where from after the demise of Allectus, future Roman emperor Constantius (Chlorus) would also administer Britain. He would also die there on 25 July 306 CE. In the restructuring programme of Allectus, more troops at this time were indicated to have been based at *Cardiff (ST18 76)*, to defend its vital military installations and to protect the Vale from both land and sea.

Part 4 The end of the British Empire

In a desperate attempt to thwart future Roman emperor Constantius (Chlorus) I, usurper Emperor Allectus burnt all his remaining ships moored in harbours along the English Channel coast. For what reason this remains uncertain, but it was probably to prevent them being captured by Constantius and subsequently used against him. However, these actions of Allectus were in vain. It was a wish, and that's all it was: to stop the army of future Roman emperor Constantius (Chlorus) before it entered mainland Europe and not on British soil. This was foiled, as the favourite general of Constantius, Asclepiodotus took a division of men to the mouth of the Seine after defeating a unit of Allectus's loyal Marine troops who had fought ineffectively. There is evidence to show that Allectus relied upon his marines, as he did not trust the loyalty of the Legions. Asclepiodotus then gathered all the ships he could find and invaded the Isle of Wight. Asclepiodotus burned all his ships on arrival to prevent them falling into the hands of Allectus, which would have given Allectus superiority.

The future Roman emperor Constantius (Chlorus) I returned to Boulogne after his earlier victories there against the usurper Emperor Allectus and prepared his invasion fleet for his remaining division of troops. Constantius landed unopposed in Kent as Allectus had been expecting the invasion via the naval bases at Porchester and Southampton, although these had been poorly prepared for such an event anyway.

Usurper Emperor Allectus was now faced with the combined forces of General Asclepiodotus and future Roman emperor Constantius (Chlorus) I. Two battlefield events had probably occurred at sites north-west of Londinium (London). Both battles ended in a resounding defeat for the forces of Allectus, and at the final battle it was believed that Allectus was taken prisoner. However, the independence of Britain from imperial Roman control was not given up easily. The remaining garrisons of Allectus (particularly in the capital Londinium itself), resisted Constantius. Only when the attempts at resistance had been over-run, did Britain once again come under direct imperial rule in 296 CE.

It is surmised that the future Emperor Constantius (Chlorus) I had ordered the destruction of military bases that had been established and re-enforced by the usurper Emperors' Carausius and Allectus, as they were deemed to pose a direct threat to Imperial authority. The prevention of any future rising by Britain and the seizing of power against Imperial Rome by remnants of the forces of Allectus (an already troubled empire threatened externally as well as internally) was, it seems, a major priority for Constantius. These actions of Constantius are believed to be seen in the decline at the *Barry harbours (ST10 66)*, and the sudden demise at the *'Official Building' Glan-y-mor (ST09 66)*, if it hadn't already been demolished on the orders of Allectus. Also any public statues of monuments erected by the usurper Emperors' Carausius and Allectus would have been slighted and thrown down. The very memory of the *'British Roman Empire eradicated from the annals of history'*.

Under the new administration of Constantius, Britain underwent a new programme of urbanisation with Londinium (London) as its capital, and self rule in towns was encouraged as well as markets, the use of the amphitheatres and general cultural sporting pursuits. This positive administrative change was greeted with open arms by the old administrators who had served under the fruitless years of former usurper Emperor Allectus.

Military and civilian life was re-organised as the whole of Britain was rejuvenated. In 296 CE the Emperors' in Rome, Diocletian and Maximianus, divided Britain into four provinces in a further attempt to make sure that uprisings under such leaders as usurper Emperors' Carausius and Allectus never recurred.

Chapter 7
The Roman 300's CE to the end of Roman Britain

Part 1 The rebuilding and demise of the late Roman Empire

This short chapter will focus on the rebuilding programme in Britain after the defeat of usurper Emperor Allectus and a few other remaining aspects.

Future Roman emperor Constantius (Chlorus) I rebuilt the walls of a number of civitas and military fortifications which were of key importance in Britain, within a refreshed spirit of 'Pax Romana'. Constantius would have certainly seen the reconstruction at the walls of *Cardiff Castle (ST18 76)*, and other important locations in the region, concentrated work on rebuilding the Hadrian's Wall frontier and other works in the north of England and Wales, with the strengthening of man-power across the British military garrisons.

The South, and South Eastern *'Saxon shore forts'* were restored and some new locations established along with signal stations. The future Emperor Constantius (Chlorus) I saw the rebuilding of the fleet, incorporating the surviving elements of *'the Squadron of the Classis Britannica'* which were now berthed in the restored harbours of the coastline. The promotion and build of cargo, passenger and supply vessels would have seen a positive change in use at harbours locally around the Bristol Channel fringe. *Caerleon (ST34 90)*, it seems, was also restored as a military base alongside its increasing urbanised vicus, but never again did it reach the height of its 100's ce prosperity. Constantius restoration of the *Cardiff (ST18 76)* Castle fort as a major base, would have brought prosperity to the Vale of Glamorgan. The Villa network would have supplied the fort. This is indicated to be the last and largest stage of redevelopment of the great fort.

Along with the changes at the end of the 200's ce and now into the new century, the Roman administration encouraged native paganism as well as other beliefs (for example Christianity) in the hope that they would be concessions leading to the strengthening of the embodiment of *'Pax Romana'*. A new period of unity flourished with Rome. Rome even made concessions so that the people of Britain (at the peak of the alien raids in the middle years of the 300's ce), could restore their nearby defences of native hill-forts for their own security. This also had another purpose; the pressure on the Roman legions across the seemingly endless frontier of the Empire was placed at breaking point. Troops were being withdrawn still further from Britain, weakening military support for the province. So eventually, even the peoples of the Vale of Glamorgan were allowed to revert to their forefather's style of native fortifications and prepare for their own protection. These Roman administrative changes may have actually been a gradual planned withdrawal by central Roman authority; to offer the Britons some safety and stability for the day Rome would withdraw all its military formations from Britain, and hence end its direct rule and sphere of influence.

Between 354 and 358 CE British Emperor Carausius II caused a further usurpation from central Roman control, although we know little to nothing of the events causing this temporary change of authority. Then shortly after, a cataclysmic disaster occurred in 367 CE when the Picts, Scots, Saxoni and Irish all invaded in quick succession, all attempting to destroy the Legions and their administration of Britain. A Roman writer, Eutropius 320 - 390 ce, (Breviarium Ab Urbe Condita *"A Brief History from the Founding of the City."*) recorded widespread destruction of villas and more humble dwellings in Britain at this time. Almost Arthurian figures, saviours like Carausius I and II would not protect Britain for a third time,

Judging by archaeological evidence from the *Llantwit Major (SS95 69)* Villa, it is believed that it was destroyed at this time, proving that the Vale would undoubtedly have been affected by the instability in the later 300's ce. As a result of all this pressure from invasions along its borders throughout the

Empire, Roman rule in the Vale abruptly ended around 407 CE, with the departure of the last Roman garrison at *Cardiff (ST18 76)*. This is when a certain Constantine III withdrew the remaining garrisons wishing to leave Britain, in his bid to become the Roman Emperor.

Part 2 The new religion of Christianity

Finally we will discuss the Christian influence in the Vale of Glamorgan, which is integral to understanding the Romans here.

At *Merthyr Mawr (SS86 76)*, there may be an early foundation for a church, as evidenced by a memorial to Paulinus who lived in the area sometime in the later 400's and early 500's ce. A number of Roman coins have been found in the area. However, this church was very open to coastal attack from pirates, as it was sited at a vulnerable location.

Irish missionaries are indicated to have come to Wales in the early 500's ce to teach of the new Christian religion, however it could equally be argued that Welsh missionaries went over to Ireland at the same time. There was more likely an exchange of ideas between Ireland and Wales. The Irish missionaries certainly would have been aware of the Christian 'teaching' establishment and religious centre at *Llantwit Major (SS96 68)*. An Irish monk named Brynach was purported to have visited Wales in the early 500's ce. Indeed, at *Llanfrynach (SS97 74)* is an isolated church which is testimony to the name of Brynach, as it is dedicated to him. The Illtyd *(Llantwit Major SS96 68)* and *Cadoc (Llancarfan ST05 70 and Cadoxton ST12 69)* monasteries would follow with other establishments which were built in the 500's ce.

However, as late as 303 CE the Romans still distrusted the influence and popularity of the Christian religion. Even though Christianisation was spreading throughout the hierarchy of the Roman world, widespread persecution was believed to still be occurring. Legend has it that Julius and Aaron, Christians from Llanharan were martyred at Caerleon for their faith.

In the Roman period, it is reputed that early saints and native aristocracy were remembered for going to Rome on pilgrimage. The legends are spread through our annals, and whichever ones have truth in them we don't know. One such story is of a certain Owain ap Cyllin being taken to Rome as a captive, and when he left his mortal body, his remains were brought back to Wales.

Reputedly St. Dubricus (Dyfrig) became the first Christian 'Bishop of Wales' known also as the Bishop of Caerleon in the 500's ce. He was purportedly known as the 'golden head' and was consecrated as a Bishop in a region of Germany. It was also recorded that in 597 ce *Llantwit Major (SS96 68)* was an established and flourishing Christian centre, indicating beyond doubt that it had a foundation date far earlier than this.

Part 3 The military withdrawal and collapse of the Roman administration in Britain

The details of the Romans leaving Britannia are obscure due to the troubled times, but here is (in part) some of the surmised evidence.

It is well established that the Romans withdrew their military from Britain in 407 CE partly due to Emperor Constantine III's bid to become Emperor, but also due to the many raids on the coastline and northern borders of Britain, and also to the fact that Rome itself was being threatened after its borders had been breached across its lengthy frontier. Every able bodied soldier was recalled from its distant provinces to retain its hold on the heart of its empire, the final defence of the city itself. Rome's aim had been to encourage the native Britannia retired soldiers, over a period of some hundred years, to become independent and to look towards its own defence as it gradually withdrew its military support. Unfortunately, the frequency of the coastal raids prevented the Roman military from withdrawing from Britain much sooner. The Roman military was expedited to defend Britain for longer.

In 400 ce, Caerwent *(ST46 90)* it is indicated was still flourishing, its stone walled defences with imposing bastions made it a formidable sanctuary. It is believed that Caerwent accepted refugees from the vulnerable coastal areas of Wales. At this time there were still garrisons left to defend civilians at Caerwent and other civitas and vici in the region. These garrisons were unlikely to be the typical roman auxiliary and legionary familiar 100 years before. They would have been composed of local Roman trained recruits led by Roman officers. A strategy of localised military defence that could have worked for many generations, except the financing of these garrisons was reliant on centralised funding as borne out in late Roman coin hoards across Britain which by 407 CE ceased to arrive, causing the Roman garrisons to disintegrate. Some late Roman coinage (Gratian 367 – 383 CE and Honorius 393 – 423 CE) have been found locally. With the maintenance of key military locations disintegrating in the region and further undermined by civilian maladministration, this would have accelerated a deterioration in law and order in the civitas and vici. Roman rule in whatever form was coming to an end

Further to the background of this military decline in 383 CE, Magnus Maximus withdrew troops from Rome's northern provinces, including the bulk of troops in Britain, in his bid to seize power in Rome. Troops were left only at principal cities and key sites such as Hadrian's Wall and Londinium (London). In 407 CE a similar action by Constantine III, caused the final withdrawal of the legions. This left the province without any legionary presence. It is currently believed that auxiliaries who wanted to stay (retiring Roman Legionaries and locally born soldiers) were the remaining military garrisons left; in effect central Rome was still administering and securing the province. However in 410 CE the last Roman officials were expelled from Britain, 'by the angry Britons'. But there is reference to a 'final' withdrawal in 412 CE of any Roman soldiers and 'officials' who wished to leave. The author cites the date 407 CE as the benchmark for the concluding chapter in centralised Roman rule in Britannia; the departure of the established 'Legions'.

However, contradictory to the reports of the military leaving Britain some 24 years earlier, local legend has it that in 436 ce a Roman army was billeted at *Colhugh harbour Llantwit Major (ST95 67)* to embark for the journey back to Rome. While they waited, they purportedly rebuilt the hill-fort's defences to protect themselves.

Thus the Romans conquered, lived, and left the Vale of Glamorgan. So was the legacy of Rome's might; *'Pax Romana'.*

Part 4 In closing

After the collapse of the Roman military and administrative control in the early 400's CE, the main threat to the Vale of Glamorgan would have been from Ireland. As early as the 200's CE, legend has it that Irish Tribes had settled in Pembrokeshire. They had been permitted to settle by the Roman administration, to offset their raids along the coast. Settlement of pirates in Britannia in the spirit of 'Pax Romana' was far more effective than the continued troublesome raids along the coast and raids against merchant shipping.

Table of peoples who have lived in the Vale of Glamorgan since 300 bce.

1. Native Peoples to 300 bce
2. Development of the three local tribes:
   East Vale of Glamorgan Coastal tribe
   West Vale of Glamorgan Coastal tribe
   Central Vale of Glamorgan tribe to 43 CE
3. Native Peoples, Romans (from all regions of the empire) to 250 ce
4. Native Peoples, Romans, Irish to 407 CE
5. Native Peoples, Romans, Irish and Germanic Peoples to 900's ce
6. The above, including Danish to 1066 CE

Thanks for reading this publication; I hope that this updated edition has assisted you with your interest in the Romans in the Vale of Glamorgan.

Glossary

Acid soil is soil with a scale pH2 to pH6 level (the level of Lemon juice has a pH2, and Vinegar has a pH3); peaty is an *Acid soil*

Aerial Photography has been extensively used throughout the latter part of the 1900's ce to discover and to understand the archaeological landscape from above

Agger the earthworks associated with the camber and revetted bank and ditch of a Roman Road

Alkaline soil is soil with a scale pH8 to pH13 levels (the level of Ammonia has a pH13, and Sea Water has a pH8.5); chalky or lime is an *Alkaline soil*

Alluvium or alluvial sediment is generally the term attributed to fine-grained clay, gravel, mud or silt usually with large amounts of organic material and archaeology that are trapped in fresh flowing water at estuaries, flood plains and river valley

Amphora large jar like containers for wine or oil storage, used for transportation of produce around the extensive Roman Empire; manufactured in vast quantities

Antonine Itinerary the Antonini Itinerarium, a contemporary Roman document that registers road distances throughout the Empire; of unknown date

Auxiliary called **Auxilia** were Subjects as opposed to *Legionaries* who were Roman citizens. Subjects were only permitted to become *Auxiliaries*; and they composed the majority of Rome's armed forces until 212 CE when all subjects became citizens

Barrow describes raised, usually circular earthworks of varying diameter that mainly contain a single or multiple *inhumation* or cremational burial. *Barrows* can range in date as a description from the middle *Neolithic* (3,500 CE), right through until recent times. Not all *Barrows* marked on maps are thus burials; some cartographers have used the word *Barrow* for example to describe a *Medieval* rabbit warren.

Bastion a projecting part of a fortification

Bloomery is a basic type of furnace for the smelting of Iron. The furnace or kiln would from processed Iron ore (Haematite), produce a *Bloom* of the refined Iron, with impurities *(Slag)* that would further be refined by re-smelting then forged into wrought iron, by beating the *slag* out whilst still molten with a hammer or press.

Brass is an alloy with principal contents as copper and zinc

Bronze principal contents are copper and tin; but other elements are included such as phosphorus, manganese, aluminium, or silicon

Bronze Age describes the period in British history from the end of the *Neolithic* in 2100 bce to the start of the *Iron Age* in 750 BCE.

Burial Chamber is generally used to refer to a *Neolithic* Long *Barrow*, but can be any stone *Built Chamber* surviving from the *Neolithic, Bronze and Iron Age.*

Bushels Measurement for Barley; one *Bushel* is approximate in modern terms to 48lbs of dried grain.

Caledonian was the name given to the generally un-conquered Scotland north of the Antonine frontier, occupied by the *Pictish* culture.

Castra, Castrum or Castellum term used for a plot of land or typically used by cartographers and historians to describe the site of a Roman Fort or other military works.

Castrametation is simply the art of laying and the construction of a Roman military fortification.

De-woodestation – a new term coined by the author for woodland that has been felled, as opposed to *De-forestation* for evergreen trees.

Cairns are possibly Burial Mounds associated with rocky landscapes. A *Cairn* can also be a non-burial stack used as a marker at promontory locations

Celt fictitious name given by the Romans to those people that occupied Britain; a clearly out of date nonsense classification. The people of Britain were a mix of settler's from the continent over a variety of different periods and native post-*Ice Age* inhabitants

Civitas Capital were locations established by the Roman administration, where native magistrates co-ordinated tax collection, local government administration, holding markets, road maintenance and so on.

Colonia particularly were seen to be a retirement town for *Legionary* soldiers and other Roman citizens wishing to settle in Britain.

Corn Dryer is a structure used extensively associated with Roman *Farmsteads*. They were used for drying grain necessary before storage and otherwise distribution

Crop marks seen through *Aerial photography*, illustrated through the different heights of crop growth also forming shadows that identify banks, ditches and other hidden earthworks.

Dark Age is now an extinct term once used by historians and archaeologists alike to describe a period in British History between the end of Roman rule 407 CE and 1066 CE. However this period is no longer Dark: with illuminated written works, a richness of *Saxon* art and artifacts, it was much lighter than the really dark period of British history: the period before the Roman invasion.

Druid fictitious name given by a variety of Roman writers to a collection of religious practices in Britian in pre-Roman times. A name perpetuated and reinforced by later historians, particularly Edward Williams (Iolo Morgannwg 10 March 1747 – 18 December 1826 CE)

Early Medieval describes the period in British history from the end of the *Roman* in 407 CE to the start of the *Medieval* in 1066CE

Earthenware is the typical word used for ceramics that have been fired at around 1000°C; termed as bisque (biscuit) also after this process was complete. Glazes are sometimes applied usually as the wheel thrown pot is still green, just before the firing process

Essyllwg Tribal area given for South Wales, a fictitious name, whose people were called the Essyllwyr by the Romans and used primarily by Ptolemy (90 – 168 CE)

Farmstead this is a unit of farm buildings and domesticated dwellings, comprising a self supporting agricultural unit, maintaining large designated tracts of land. Roman *farmsteads* were usually attached to a network co-ordinated by a centralised *Villa*. *Farmstead* tenants attempted to emulate their *Villa* masters accommodation; with limited areas heated by a *Hypocaust*, occasional *Tessellated paving*, and most certainly *Corn-Drying kilns*

Fibulae is a Roman brooch, typically for fastening clothing, and made from all metals in many shapes and forms

Field Pattern - Archaeological term for field boundaries, ploughing and other agricultural activity such as stock control

Flint Mineral Quartz Stone formed into nodules within chalk. Can be found washed up on our shore, but is usually of poor quality for processing

Flue tiles or Box flue tiles are part of the central heating system of a Roman hypocaust. These 'tiles' channel warm air through regular vertical cavities underneath the plastered internal render.

Fortlet A small fort usually containing fewer than 500 Roman soldiers.

Garrison a unit of soldiers dwelling in a fortification.

Garum was fermented fish sauce made from crushing and fermentation in brine of the innards of various fish such as eel, mackerel,tuna, and others - used extensively in Roman cuisine cooking.

Gauls is the historical name given mainly for the people that inhabited France and outlying countries before and throughout the Roman period. *Gaul*

is famous for Gaius Julius Caesars 'Gallic campaign', it eventually became three provinces of the Roman world: Gallia

Gordel Raids were alleged coastal incursions by the *'Gordel'*, along South Wales several centuries before the Roman invasion of 43 CE

Half life of pebbles the time it would take for pebbles to reduce by half their original size

Hill-forts are earthworks built from the late *Bronze Age* onwards usually as *Univallatte* leading through to the end of the *Iron Age* as *Multivallate* type. Initially *Hill-forts* were used as secure grain storage and animal storage compounds, then onto defensive sanctuaries at the start of the Roman invasion.

Hoards are usually classed as coins of any denomination and date that are in excess of 8 in quantity.

Homestead is similar to a *Farmstead* in that it is a self supporting unit of occupation with a dwelling, and occasional out-buildings. A *Homestead* is however much smaller than its counterpart, without all of the same functions and farm out-buildings and can be found in villages

Ice Age the last of which was in full retreat by 12,000 years ago, it is believed to have started 110,000 years ago; it is scientifically referred to as the Pleistocene

Igneous rock unlike *sedimentary rock* has been created through the solidification of magma and lava. Certain types of *Igneous rocks* are granite and rhyolite

Imbrex are the standard semi circular earthenware tiles used in roof construction to crown the joint-overlaps between the *Tegulae*; plural *Imbrices*

Inhumation is the standard burial practice, as opposed to a cremation.

Iron Age describes the period from the end of the *Bronze Age* in 750 bce to the start of the Roman in 43 CE.

Iron Slag material left over from the iron smelting process

Land Tenure An allotted area of land producing income, and to 'hold' the land as a tenant as *Land Tenure* from the owner.

Legionary most notable for their curved shield, short sword: gladius, and plate armour. Initially only Roman citizens from Italy could be a *Legionary*, and were typically not permitted to marry. *Legionaries* were usually paid adequate and varying amounts for their service, and may typically serve 25 years and settled with a grant of land at a *Colonia* for ex-servicemen. However this would all change in 212 CE as requirements for a Legionary, enabled them to marry, and to be Roman citizens from outside Italy.

Loam is soil with a composition of sand, silt (and humus) and clay to a ratio of 40-40-20%. This composition for Loam allows it to retain water, but also to drain at an appropriate rate for agriculture

Mansio is usually the description given for an 'overnight' official stopping place on a Roman road, there are no locations identified along our *Via Julia Maritima*

Marching Camp a standard construct of the campaigning Roman army. The requirement to construct a Temporary camp (also referred with that name by cartographers) after each days march. The 'camp' would have had a complete rampart, ditch, palisade (each soldier carried 2 stakes for this) and up to 4 clavicula (curved internal or external entrances). Usually maintained for more than one night, to accommodate supplies, and other troops for the advancing army

Medieval describes the period in British history from the end of the *Early Medieval* in 1066 CE to the start of the *Post-Medieval* in 1485 CE

Mesolithic describes the period in British history from the end of the *Upper Palaeolithic* in 8,500 bce to the start of the *Neolithic* in 4,250 bce

Mesozoic Jurassic Lias Limestone most common local underlying Geology, a period dating from 200 – 145 millions years old, useful for creating lime and building

Mortarium is the standard kitchen vessel, popularly with heavy fabric and flange (rim), usually as courseware typically for grinding down ingredients for recipes, plural *Mortaria*

Multivallate a *Hill-fort* with more than one set of banks and ditches

Neolithic describes the period in British history from the end of the *Mesolithic* in 4250 bce to the start of the *Bronze Age* in 2100 BCE.

Neutral soil is soil with a scale pH7 level (the level of Milk has a pH6.5); clay is a *Neutral soil*.

Ogham script was popular between 300's – 600's CE, up to 25 characters in any set Ogham alphabet as a series of lines. On standing stones, over 500 known across Britain and Ireland.

Opus Signinum this is usually used as a hard base in construction, typically with broken tile and other aggregate mixed with mortar and rammed into wooden framed patterns and set for structures

Palaeozoic Carboniferous Lias Limestone local underlying Geology, a period dating from 360 – 300 millions years old, useful for building.

Palisade is a tight arrangement of wooden or stone defense work, raised above a bank to create extra height and protection for defenders.

Pax Romana Latin for "Roman peace", it is mainly used to describe episodes throughout the empire when there was relative stability, and little external warfare.

Pennant Sandstone is often referred to as the Upper Coal Measures; this is a sequence of *Sedimentary rocks* typical of the South Wales Coalfield. Slabs made of this material are used for flooring or roofing.

Pharos a Roman lighthouse, term derives from The *Pharos* of Alexandria in Egypt.

Picts were the distinctive cultural name given to the north eastern people of Scotland for the period of Roman conquest that was taking place further south; term used until the emergence of the Scottish nation states in the *Medieval*

Pilae are square earthenware tiles stacked up at regular intervals to allow warm air to circulate, and then support the flooring in Roman rooms

Ploughshare is the blade made of wood or metal that creates the furrow for cultivation

Post- Medieval describes the period in British history from the end of the *Medieval* in 1485 CE, right through until the start of the Industrial Revolution in Britain in 1750 CE.

Practice Works are Roman earthworks used for training its military. These earthworks are not always complete, and take many forms of linear works, clavicula and corner bastions.

Quicklime or calcium oxide is often referred to as burnt lime or simply lime; the product of heating up refined *Lias Limestone* under intense temperatures in a charcoal fired Limekiln.

Radiate crown *see, Chapter 3 the activities of Roman occupation and religion Part 2 Exports, imports and coinage.*

Red Radyr Sandstones is a *Mesozoic Triassic Sedimentary rock* (created 250 – 200 years ago). It was first identified in the late 1800's ce by John Storrie, also known by its standard name of Old Red Sandstone

Samian or Terra Sigillata, its Latin term, which was used for red glossed Roman pottery produced mainly in *Gaul* (Mainly modern day France), Germania (mainly modern day Germany) and Italy. Hans Dragendorff.in 1896 identified potteries and its different types, and gave the time frame from the 0's bce - 250 ce as dates for its manufacture and popularity

Saxoni or the Saxons were the primary Germanic tribal group offered settlement terms in Britain by the Romans in 300's CE, simply after the Roman occupation they were to take over as the predominant authority in vast parts of Britain by the 600's CE.

Sedimentary layers are deposited as strata forming beds under intense pressure. *Sedimentary rock* is very unlike *Igneous* and *Metamorphic. Types of Sedimentary rock* are Limestone, Mudstone and Sandstone

Shale is fine-grained *Sedimentary rock,* usually containing clay, minerals and quartz. Shale is found through coal mining, and along beach margin outcrops. It can be typically black, earthly colours, various buff colours, red, green and so on.

Signal Station are usually square towers with ancillary buildings established for warning and signalling instructions. Usually a faggot is burnt on a raised iron basket, or on a stone base. If built inland they are used for military instructions and for warning of impending danger. Similarly they are used at regular intervals along the coast to assist the 'Classis Britannica'

Silures fictious name given by the Romans to the group of tribes across South Wales and Gloucestershire.

Tegula are the standard earthenware flat pan tiles used in roofing with the raised flanged overlaps on two sides covered by the *Imbrex.* Plural: *Tegulae*

Tessellate or Roman *Tessellated* paving are usually laid down in long corridors with less ornate panels than standard 'Mosaic' work within rooms at Roman 'status' sites (such as *villas*). *Tesserae* are the small cubes of *Limestone, Sandstone,* marble or other stone and tile used to construct the *Tessellated* paving or 'mosaic.'

Topography describing the physical geographical features of a place or location.

Tumuli name given to a raised earthen, sometimes stone burial mound with an extensive date range, basically a *Barrow.*

Univallate this is similar to a *Multivallate hill-fort* in the *Iron-Age,* but with one key difference, in that it only has one set of defences (bank and ditch), usually constructed from the late *Bronze Age,* through to the middle *Iron Age.*

Vallum the set of defences around a fortification.

Vicus civilian suburb of a Roman fort or town, or simply a village. *Vici* as plural.

Villa a Roman rural civilian administration centre to co-ordinate a large estate of *Farmsteads* and small communities, used to: accommodate the local elite's family, workforce, with bath block, mosaics, *Tessellated* paving, central heating, frescoes, usually with roof tiles of *Pennant sandstone* stabs, and luxury rooms and accommodation. Used for status, storage of produce and for Tax collection

Wattle and Daub are the upright panels used in building. The *Wattle* is created from a frame of birch, made then from interwoven: hazel, or willow, to create a hurdle. This is then placed into position with *Daub*: usually a mix of soil, clay, sand, animal dung, water (and urine) and most importantly straw, hay or horse hair to bond

Yield an amount of a unit of cultivated agricultural product.

Dating system used in this publication:
CE Common Era (non-Christian name used by other religion based authors for AD or Anno Domini)
BCE Before Common Era (non-Christian name used by other religion based authors for BC or Before Christ)
bce un-calibrated date, the same as BC, although the date is based on speculation, hearsay, or historical evidence and not calibrated scientific techniques such as Dendrochronology or Radio Carbon Dating
CE un-calibrated date, the same as CE, *see above*

Coinage types used in this publication
See, **Chapter 3 the activities of Roman occupation and religion**
Part 2 Exports, imports and coinage

Military formations and leaders used in this publication such as: Auxilia, Alae, Centurion, Cohorts, Decurion, Praefectus and Turmae, *see,* **Part 4 Local typology, military occupation and military formations**

Chronology of selected Roman Emperors' (with important Caesars and Empress) and Usurper Emperors' derivatives
Chronology with coin finds in the Vale of Glamorgan (Number of coins not specified at locations, single coins classed the same as a hoard) indicated site in italics *(example Barry).*

BRITISH or GALLIC Refers in the latter to the usurper Emperors' for the British and Gaul Empire on 2 occasions and in the former refers to the *Germania, Gaul, Britannia,* and *Hispania* break-away empire.

. . .+2 Refers to the Emperors' not mentioned in this chronology, usually those Emperors' in some cases who reigned for a matter of weeks.

Emperor	When Proclaimed, then date of Death, Abdication or murder (dates all in CE)

Claudius I   25 January 41 - 13 October 54
Barry Birchgrove Wood, Bridgend, Cowbridge, Llantwit Major, St. Brides-Super-Ely

Nero   13 October 54 - 9 June 68
Llantwit Major, Monknash, St. Brides-Super-Ely

Clodius Macer   April 68 - October 68

Galba   9 June 68 - 15 January 69
Monknash

Otho   15 Jan 69 - 17 April 69
Monknash

Vitellius   2 January 69 – 20 December 69
Monknash

Vespasian   1 July 69 - 24 June 79
Bonvilston, Boverton, Cardiff, Eglwys Brewis, Llantwit Major, Monknash, Ogmore, St. Brides-Super-Ely

Titus   24 June 79 - 13 September 81
Monknash

Domitian   13 September 81 - 18 September 96
Boverton, Cowbridge, Monknash, Whitton Lodge

Nerva   18 September 96 - 25 January 98
Bonvilston, Boverton, Ely, Monknash

Trajan   25 January 98 - 8 August 117
Biglis, Bonvilston, Boverton, Cowbridge, Eglwys Brewis, Ely, Monknash, Whitton Lodge

Marciana   105 - 112
Monknash

Hadrian   *8 August 117 - 10 July 138*
Bonvilston, Cowbridge, Eglwys Brewis, Marcross, Michaelston le pit, Monknash, St. Brides-Super-Ely, Whitton Lodge

Sabina   8 August 117 - – early 137
Monknash

Antoninus Pius   10 July 138 - 7 March 161
Bonvilston, Boverton, Cardiff, Cowbridge, Eglwys Brewis, Ely, Laleston, Monknash, Porthcawl, St. Brides-super-Ely

Faustina   10 July 138 – early 141
Monknash

Marcus Aurelius   7 March 161- 17 March 180
Biglis, Cardiff

Lucius Verus   7 March 161 - Early 169

Commodus   177 - 31 December 192

Pertinax   1 January 193 - 28 March 193

Didius Julianus   28 March 193 - 2 June 193

Pescennius Niger   April 193 – Autumn 194

Clodius Albinus   Autumn 195 - 19 February 197

Septimius Severus   13 April 193 - 4 February 211

Caracalla   Early 198 - 8 April 217

Geta	Autumn 209 - 1 February 212
Macrinus	11 April 217 - June 218 . . .+1
Elagabalus	16 May 218 - 6 March 222
Severus Alexander	6 March 222 - March 235
Corntown	
Maximinus I	March 235 - 24 June 238
Ewenny	
Gordian (Africanus) I	22 March 238 - 12 April 238
Gordian (Africanus) II	22 March 238 - 12 April 238 . . .+2
Gordian III	29 July 238 - 25 February 244
Philip I	25 February 244 - September 249
Philip II	May 247 – September 249. . .+2
Trajan Decius	Sept 249 - June 251 ...+2
Trebonianus Gallus	June 251 - Summer 253...+2
Aemilian	Summer - 253 – Autumn 253
St. Donat's	
Valerian	September 253 - June 260
Gallienus	September 253 - August 268...+4

Barry Island St. Barruc's, Biglis, Cardiff, Llantwit Major, Whitton Lodge

Claudius (Gothicus) II	August 268 - January 270...+1
Biglis, Whitton Lodge	
Aurelian	April 270 - April 275 ...+2
Cardiff	
Probus	May 276 - Autumn 282 ...+1
Carus	Autumn 282 - August 283...+3
GALLIC Postumus	259 - Late 268...+1
Biglis, Cardiff, Llandough, Llanfair	
GALLIC Marius	Late 268 – Early 269
St. Donat's	
GALLIC Victorinus	Early 269 - 270
Barry Glan-y-mor, Biglis, Cardiff, Llantwit Major	
GALLIC Tetricus I	270 - Late 273
Biglis, Cardiff, Llantwit Major, Ogmore	
GALLIC Tetricus II	273 - Autumn 274 ...+1
Biglis, Cardiff, Whitton Lodge	
BRITISH Carausius	late 286 - 293

Biglis, Cardiff, Colhugh Hill-fort, Ely, Llantwit Major, Sully Moor, Whitton Lodge

BRITISH Allectus	293 - 296
Barry Glan-y-mor, Biglis, Sully Moors	
Diocletian	20 Nov 284 - 1 May 305
Maximianus	April 286 - 1 May 305 ...+1
Ewenny, Marcross	
	November 306 - November 308
	Spring 310 - Spring 310
Constantius (Chlorus) I	1 May 305 - 25 July 306
Barry Glan-y-mor, Biglis	
Severus II	25 July 306 - Summer 307
Maximianus (Galerius) II	1 May 305 – May 311

Whitton Lodge

Maximinus II	Early 309 - Autumn 313
Maxentius	28 October 306 - 28 October 312 ...+1
Licinius	November 308 - Autumn 324 ...+2
Constantine (Great) I	Spring 307 - 22 May 337

Biglis, Cardiff, Cosmeston, Cowbridge, Ely, Llanbethery, Ogmore, Peterston-Super-Ely

Flavius Dalmatius	19 September 335 - Summer 337
Helena	337 – 341

Whitton Lodge

Constantine II	9 September 337 - Spring 340

Whitton Lodge

Constans I	9 September 337 - Early 350

Biglis, Llancarfan, Peterston Super Ely, St. Brides-Super-Ely, St. Lythans

Constantius II	9 September 337 - 3 November 361

Biglis, Caermead

Magnentius	18 January 350 – 11 August 353 ...+2
BRITISH Carausius II	354 - 358
Julian II	Early 360 – 26 June 363...+1
Valentinian I	26 February 364 - 17 November 375

Aberthaw, Biglis, Penmark

Valens	28 March 364 - 9 August 378...+1
Gratian	24 August 367 - 25 August 383

Cardiff

Valentinian II	22 November 375 - 15 May 392
Theodosius (The Great) I	19 January 379 - 17 January 395
Magnus Maximus	July 383 - 28 July 388 ...+2
Arcadius	19 Jan 383 - 1 May 408
Honorius	10 Jan 393 - 25 Aug 423

Cardiff

Constantine III	407 - September 411
Constans II	408 - Early 411
Maximus	409 - 411

Radiate coins were imitation coins from the late 200's ce, produced by the western provinces and usurper Emperors', to supplement the dwindling coinage issued by the central mints of the empire, mainly of Antoninianus coinage.

Biglis, Palmerston Barry, Whitton Lodge

GLORIA EXERCITVS (Glory of the Army) type coins were issued by the emperor reigns of: Constantine I, Constans, Constantine II, Constantius II, Delmatius and through anonymous city issues between 307-361 CE it is believed to commemorate the role that the military played across the empire. Large quantities of these bronze coins were minted.

Barry

Coins in the original publication referred to only as coin finds in the *'Sites Index'*, have been deleted from the above list. It is not appropriate to include coins that may not in fact be Roman in period; and by the very fact they haven't been positively identified, adds to speculation to their origins. Lastly every coin find has to be judged with some sceptism; afterall anyone visiting continental Europe may pick up a coin in a market, and subsequently loose it in their garden (it's context lost).

200's ce Aberkenfig, Cardiff, Pyle (notable across range finds)

Gazetteer of visible Roman remains or artefacts mentioned in the text; or not mentioned if the case may be, that enhance this books 'experience' in the local vicinity.

This is a recommended gazetteer of generally accessible Roman sites and collections visible in the region between the river Usk and river Neath, south of Merthyr Tydfil. Although we concede we may not have listed every accessible site in the region hereby mentioned; as many are on private land and at locations and times there is a closure of footpaths - they are overgrown (summer months) and it would be unwise for the author to suggest a visit.

Opening times and access arrangements are current at time of 2010, second edition publication.

Road sections:
Narrow stretch at *Gelligaer Common* running towards survey marker, the archaeology is defined by the remains of an enclosing drainage ditch. Free access *(SO10 03)*

Agger and camber visible at *St. Hilary Down.* The drainage ditch of the Agger to south facing is particularly distinctive. Free access *(ST01 73)*

Military:
Fort ground plan outlined by Red Radyr Sandstone and display at *Cardiff Castle.* The Roman walls can be viewed from outside the castle, but access within is advisable to view the thickness of the wall, and display. Payable

access. Open times: 9.00 – 17.00 everyday Castle St., Cardiff CF10 3RB, Wales. Tel: 029 2087 8100 (ST18 76)

Fort at **Neath.** Two conserved and displayed gateway for the south east and south west. Both gateways are fenced off; the South east gateway is by far well worth a visit. Free access (SS74 97)

Fort and Practice works at **Gelligaer.** The outline walls, and earthworks, and a lot of imagination can make this site a worthwhile visit. Free access (ST13 97)

Fortress and Vicus at **Caerleon.** The remains of the Amphitheatre, Barrack blocks, Fortress Walls, Baths (under cover), Museum and occasional summer excavations and re-enactment displays. Of particular importance to the visitor is the Amphitheatre, but likewise the other remains and collections at the Museum are on par. Free and Payable access. Opening times vary. Tel: 01633 423 134 (ST34 90)

Official Building **Cold Knap, Barry.** The remains of 90% of the original floor plan are on display with a basic history of the site. Beware of the inaccurate portrayal of the site; as the display boards discuss and maintain that there was only one phase of construction on site. Free access (ST09 66)

Museums:

Newport Museum and Galleries. There are a variety of artifacts on display. Free access. Open times: 0900-1600 (longer for most days) Monday to Saturday John Frost Square Newport NP20 1PA. Tel: 01633 656656 (ST31 87)

Cowbridge Museum. The displays are limited; as most of the Roman material once on offer have been taken to the National Museum and will probably never be placed on public display again, but the colourful floor plan of mosaic from Caermead is well worth it. Donation advisable. Open times: 1100-1600 1st Sat in Month Town Hall Cells, Town Hall, High Street, Cowbridge, Vale Of Glamorgan, CF71 7DD. Tel: 01446 775139 (SS99 74)

National Museum and Galleries of Wales. The once extensive collection of Roman material on display at Wales's main museum is no longer available, but the material that is available is a valuable resource in understanding the Roman occupation. Free access (at present). Open times: 10.00-17.00 Tuesday to Sunday Cathay's Park, Cardiff, South Glamorgan CF10 3NP. Tel: 029 2039 7951 (ST18 76)

Margam Stones Museum. Has a small but well presented and accessible display of Standing Stones from the late Roman period through to the Medieval. Payable access. Open Times: 10.30 - 16.00 Wednesday to Sunday (April to September for access outside this period contact the custodian). Tel: 01639 871184 (SS 80 86)

The authors private collection of Roman artefacts. Can be viewed through arrangement with the author.

The inventory of sites and non-coin finds

This inventory of sites and non-coin finds referred to in this publication, will be extensively revised in edition three. But for now, please take the entries as accurate at their time of original publication in 1996 and some author additions since. Only four figure references are given to protect some of the locations exact identity

Italics – projected of surmised artefacts and sites (with a 50% margin of error). Due to hearsay, lost records, these artefacts and sites we are unable to calibrate

Bold – identified Roman findings and sites (with a 10% margin of error)

Bold and underlined – definite Roman sites

Artefacts - Variety of artefacts recorded at these locations of probable Roman date, and were unspecified artefacts in much of the research sources, also any structures illustrated here are all indicative of artefact assemblage particularly, but are classed as *'Artefacts'* due to walls and other structural remains being illusive to date

Buildings- Would be indicated through archaeological techniques such as aerial photography, excavation, concentrations of artefacts etc...

Concentrated evidence in certain area's (Barry for example) only indicates intensive field work by archaeologists which offers us a biased over view for that location, this does in no means give a full accurate level of occupation for the region

*Blue Glass Bead distribution is recorded in the site index, due to a personal interest of this anomaly by the author

Aberthaw	ST03 66	*Harbour, Building*
Aberthaw	ST03 66	Building
Atlantic Trading Estate	ST13 67	Glass, *Glass cremation jars,*
(Bendricks)		**Burials**
(and surrounds)		*Lead coffin, Five stone lined burials*
Barry	ST08 66	*Harbour*
(Westward Corner)	ST09 66	*Buildings, Quarry*
(Glan-y-mor)	ST09 66	**Official Building**
	ST09 66	*Burial*
(Cwm Barri)	ST09 67	*Artefacts*
(Cwm Cidi)	ST09 67	*Wells*
	ST09 69	**Artefacts**

	ST10 66	**Artefacts**
(Cold Knap)	ST10 66	*Building, Harbour*
(St. Nicholas Ch.)	ST10 66	*Artefacts*
(Old Harbour)	ST10 66	*Harbour,* **Artefacts**
(Barry Castle)	ST10 67	**Building**
	ST10 67	*Artefacts*
	ST10 68	*Well*
(Merthyr Dyfan)	ST11 69	Artefacts, Well
	ST12 69	*Building*
(Daniel Street)	ST12 69	**Blue Glass Beads, Artefacts*
(Pencoetre)	ST12 70	*Corn Drying Kiln*
	ST13 69	*Sword*
(Victoria Park)	ST13 69	**Building**
	ST13 69	*Building*
(Palmerston)	ST14 69	*Building*
Barry Island	ST11 66	*Artefacts*
(St. Peirio's Abbey)	ST11 66	*Building*
	ST11 66	*Well*
	ST11 66	*Fibula, Samian*
(St. Barruc's Ch.)	ST11 66	*Artefacts, Loom Weight*
Biglis	ST14 69	**Building, Settlement, Burials, Corn Drying Kilns,** **Blue Glass Beads*
	ST14 69	*Artefacts*
Bonvilston	ST06 74	*Lamp*
Boverton	SS98 68	*Building*
Bridgend	SS89 78	*Military*
	SS90 78	*Military*
Cae Summerhouse	SS99 66	**Settlement,** Corn Drying Kilns
Caer Dynnaf	SS98 74	*Quern stone, Building*
Candleston Castle	SS87 77	*Artefacts*
Cardiff	ST14 76	***Villa***
	ST15 77	*Building*
	ST17 78	*Building*
	ST18 76	**Fort**
	ST19 78	*Building*
(Llanederyn)	ST19 81	***Pottery kiln,*** *Artefacts*
(Rumney)	ST20 78	*Military*
Castle-upon-Alun	SS91 74	*Burials, Military artefacts*
Colwinston	SS93 76	*Artefacts*
Corntown	SS91 77	*Artefacts*
	SS92 76	*Building*
	SS93 76	*Building*
	SS93 76	*Agriculture*
Cosmeston	*SS17 68*	*Building*
Cowbridge	SS98 74	*Building*
	SS99 74	**Bovium Fort, Burials**
	SS99 74	**Buildings of Vicus and road**

	SS99 74	Artefacts, Corn Dryer, Industrial Activity
	SS99 74	Military **Ornamental Sculpture (Lion)**
	SS98 74	*Building*
	SS97 75	*Agriculture*
	SS98 75	*Crop Marks*
Dan-y-Graig	SS84 78	*Building, Corn Dryer*
Dinas Powys	ST15 69	*Building*
	ST15 70	*Building*
	ST15 69	*Artefacts*
	ST15 70	*Buildings,* **Artefacts,** *Crop marks* **Blue Glass Bead, iron Smelting, Agriculture*
Dunraven	SS88 72	*Building*
Eglwys Brewis	ST00 69	*Artefacts*
Ewenny	SS91 77	*Artefacts*
	SS90 77	*Crop marks*
	SS90 77	*Artefacts*
(Priory)	SS91 77	*Military, Burials, Building, Fibula*
Flat Holm	ST22 64	*Artefacts*
Heol y Mynydd	SS88 75	*Building*
Kenfig	SS80 80	*Artefacts*
	SS82 78	*Artefacts*
	SS84 77	*Artefacts*
Laleston	SS87 79	*Building*
Lavernock	ST17 67	*Building*
Llanbethery	ST03 70	**Building**
Llanblethian	SS98 74	*Quern, Building*
	SS99 74	*Building*
Llancadle	ST03 68	*Artefacts, Burials*
Llancarfan	ST05 70	*Artefacts*
	ST03 70	*Building*
Llandough	ST16 73	**Building, Burials**
Llandough	ST16 73	**Cemetery**
Llanfrynach	SS97 74	*Building*
Llangan	SS96 77	*Artefacts, Burial*
Llanmaes	SS98 69	*Artefacts*
Llanmihangel	SS98 71	*Building*
Llantrithyd	ST03 73	*Quern, Artefacts*
	ST04 72	*Artefact*
Llantwit Major	SS96 68	*Burial*
(Caermead)	SS96 69	**Villa, Burials**
	SS96 67	*Artefacts*
	SS96 67	*Harbour*
Llysworney	SS97 75	*Building*
	SS96 74	*Building*
Maes y Ward	ST02 74	*Quern, Building*
Margam	SS85 77	*Artefact, Burial, Building*

	SS86 76	*Artefacts*
	SS86 77	*Artefact*
	SS86 78	*Artefacts*
Merthyr Mawr	SS86 76	*Artefacts*
Monknash	SS91 69	*Building*
Moulton	ST07 69	**Building**
	ST07 69	Building
	ST07 69	*Building*
Nash Manor	SS96 73	*Artefacts*
Newton	SS84 77	*Building*
Nottage	SS82 78	*Artefacts, Burials*
Nurston	ST05 67	*Building, Industrial activity*
Ogmore	SS88 76	*Military Artefacts*
Ogmore Down	SS89 76	*Military*
Old Castle Down	*SS90 75*	*Military*
Penarth	ST18 72	*Artefacts*
Penllyn	SS97 76	*Buildings*
Penmark	ST05 68	Crop marks
	ST05 68	*Artefacts*
	ST05 67	*Artefacts*
	ST05 67	*Building*
	ST05 68	*Agriculture*
Pen-y-lan	ST19 78	*Buildings*
Pop Hill	ST15 70	*Agriculture, Buildings, *Blue glass Bead*
Porthcawl	SS80 77	*Artefacts*
	SS80 78	*Artefacts*
	SS84 76	*Artefacts*
Porthkerry	ST07 66	*Buildings*
(Bullhouse)	ST07 67	*Well*
(Castle Rock)	ST08 65	*Pharos*
(The Bulwarks)	ST08 66	**Building**
	ST08 66	*Harbour*
	ST08 66	*Building*
	ST08 67	*Artefacts*
	ST09 67	*Building, Glass*
Pyle	SS82 79	*Artefacts*
Rhoose	ST07 67	*Artefacts*
St. Andrews Major	ST13 72	*Artefacts*
St. Brides Major	SS88 75	*Agriculture*
	SS89 75	*Agriculture*
St. Brides-Super-Ely	ST09 78	*Military Artefacts, Artefacts*
St. Donat's Castle	ST93 68	*Artefacts*
St. Hilary	ST02 74	*Artefacts*
St. Hilary	ST01 74	*Artefacts*
St. Hilary	ST01 73	**Road**
St. Lythans	ST10 72	*Artefacts*
Southerndown	SS89 72	*Agriculture*
Sully	ST15 68	*Artefacts*

(Castle)	ST15 68	*Artefacts*
	ST16 67	*Artefacts*
Summerhouse Point	SS99 66	Artefacts
Swanbridge	ST16 67	*Crop marks*
Wenvoe (Goldsland)	ST10 71	*Lead mining, Building*
	ST11 71	*Lead mining, Buildings*
	ST12 73	*Buildings*
	ST12 74	*Artefacts*
Whitelands (West Ridge)	ST08 67	**Artefacts**
Whitton	ST08 71	Buildings
(Lodge)	ST08 71	**Villa (Mansio), Well, *Blue glass beads**
	ST08 72	Building
Wick	SS91 73	*Building*
	SS92 73	*Artefacts*

Bibliography and Credits
Principal published works consulted
With Articles and monographs

Anon 1986 Archaeology in Wales Volume 26 Council for British Archaeology
Anon (uncited) The Bulletin of the Board of Celtic Studies Volume IV 1927 - 1929
Anon 1926 Transactions of the Cardiff Naturalists' Society Volume LIX
Anon 1933 Transactions of the Cardiff Naturalists' Society Volume LXVI
Askew G 1951 The coinage of Roman Britain
Awbery S (uncited) Names and their origins in Barry and the Vale
Awbery S 1954 Let us talk of Barry
Awbery S 1965 I searched for Llantwit Major
Awbrey S 1959 The Story of St. Athan and Aberthaw
Awbrey S 1967 St. Donat's Castle and the Stradlings
Cadw 1987 Ancient Monuments and Archaeological Areas Act 1979: Schedule of Monuments of National Importance: the Counties of Mid South and West Glamorgan As at 1 January 1988
Carson R A G 1980 Principal Coins of Romans - Volume II - the Principate, 31BC - AD 296
Davies C & Dykes D W 1981 Alan Sorrell: Early Wales Re-created
Dowdell G 1980 The Glamorgan Gwent Archaeological Trust Annual Report 1979 - 1980
Dowdell G & Savory H 1982 The Glamorgan Gwent Archaeological Trust Annual Report 1981 - 1982
Dowdell G 1983 The Glamorgan Gwent Archaeological Trust Annual Report 1982 - 1983
Ewbank T 1921 The Geography & History of Barry
Fletcher E 1977 Treasure Hunting on the Coast
Fox A 1936 An account of John Storrie's excavation on Barry Island 1894-5
Gilbert A 1967 The Coinage of Roman Britain
Jarrett V E & Nash-Williams M G 1967 The Frontier in Wales
Jarrett M G & Wrathmell S 1981.Whitton: An Iron Age and Roman Farmstead in South Glamorgan
Jones J I 1956 An Atlas of Wales Part One Geographical
Jones D M (undated) Search for Bomium Field work of a local archaeologist
Jones D M (undated) Search for Bomium A Local History of Bridgend and Surrounding Villages bridged to Search for Bomium Part Two Field work of a local archaeologist
Hawkes J 1986 The Shell Guide to British Archaeology
Leland J 1769 A Booke of Glamorganshires Antiquities By Rice Merrick Esq 1578. In, Corbett J A 1972 (ed.), *The Itinerary of John Leland* : 131
Lloyd-Jones M 1984 Society and Settlement in Wales and the Marches (British Archaeological Reports (BAR))
Francis D J 1976 Border Vale of Glamorgan
Luxton B C 1980 St. Cadoc's: a History of the Old Village Church Cadoxton-Juxta-Barry
Luxton B 1977 Old Barry in Photographs I
Luxton B 1978 Old Barry in Photographs II
Luxton B 1990 Old Barry in Photographs III
Margary I D 1973 Roman Roads in Britain 3rd edition
Moore D (Ed) 1985 Barry The Centenary Book
Morris A 1923 Glamorgan: Being an Outline of Its Geography, History, and Antiquities with Maps and Illustrations
Nash-Williams V E 1953 The Roman villa at Llantwit Major in Glamorgan
Robinson D M 1980 Cowbridge: The Archaeology and Topography of a Small Market Town in the Vale of Glamorgan (Town survey)
Robinson D M 1985 South Glamorgan's Heritage
Royal Commission on Ancient and Historical Monuments in Wales 1976 An Inventory of the Ancient Monuments in Glamorgan Volume 1 part 2, The Iron age and Roman Occupation
Sear D R 1987 The Emperors' of Roman and Byzantium
Storrie J (uncited) Transactions of the Cardiff Naturalists' Society 1888 - 1890
Storrie J (uncited) Transactions of the Cardiff Naturalists' Society 1891 -1895
Storrie J (uncited) Transactions of the Cardiff Naturalists' Society 1895 - 1896

Storrie J (uncited) Transactions of the Cardiff Naturalists' Society 1896 - 1897
Storrie J (uncited) Transactions of the Cardiff Naturalists' Society 1897 - 1902
Storrie J & Watson W 1896 Notes on Excavations made during the summers of 1894-5, at Barry Island and Ely Race Course, on lands the property of the Right Honourable Lord Windsor. With illustrations
Williams S 1963 Glamorgan Historian Volume One
Williams S 1965 Glamorgan Historian Volume Two
Williams S 1966 Glamorgan Historian Volume Three
Williams S 1967 Glamorgan Historian Volume Four
Williams S 1968 Glamorgan Historian Volume Five
Williams S 1969 Glamorgan Historian Volume Six
Williams S 1959 Vale Of Glamorgan Series Volume 1 History On My Doorstep
Williams S 1973 Volume 2 Vale Of History
Williams S 1973 Volume 3 The Garden Of Wales
Williams S 1973 Volume 4 Saints And Sailing Ships
Wilson R J A 1988 A guide to the Roman Remains in Britain
Wilson D R 1967 Roman Frontiers of Britain
Wyman B 2005 Treasure Islands Britain's History Uncovered

Newspapers

South Wales Echo newspaper, 29th September,1963; Dinas Powys and The Romans
The Barry Dock News ,1890, 1891, 1892, 1893, 1894, 1895, 1897, 1898,
The Barry and District Newspaper, 1965

Maps

Booth J 1978 Antique Maps of Wales
Ordnance Survey 1913 England and Wales sheet 263 (3rd edition)
Ordnance Survey 1962 Land use sheet 194
Ordnance Survey 1977 Barry ST 06/16 1:25 000 Second Series
Ordnance Survey 1978 Map of the Roman Britain Maps; South sheet
Ordnance Survey 2001 Roman Britain Historical Map (5th edition)

Artefact, Document and record sources (to 1996)

Barry Library
Cardiff Library
Glamorgan-Gwent Archaeological Trust Ltd. Sites Monuments Record, Swansea
National Museum and Galleries of Wales, Cardiff
Mid with South Glamorgan Records Office
Storrie J (various uncited) Personal Archive on Porthkerry and Barry at Mid with South Glamorgan Records Office, Cardiff
Swansea Museum
Williams E (Iolo Morgannwg) (various uncited) notes 1746-1826

Unpublished

Welsh Young Archaeology Society
Welsh Archaeological Institute
Archaeology Cymru Consultancy Ltd

Acknowledgements

Michael Jenkins
Howard J Thomas

Annex to second edition
Other acknowledgements in 2014

Lisa Hillyard for encouragement and giving me the push to complete this edition. My various students for their loyalty and encouragement to complete this work, and assisting me with field work. Ivan Parker for the support in this undertaking. Proof Reading thanks to Ryland Morgan, Ivan Parker, Adam Van Doorninck and Cathy Richards. The Artwork is by Nicole Hay.